Augsburg College
George Sverdrup Library
Minneapolis, Minnesota 55404

WITHDRAWN

THE RISE OF URBAN AMERICA

ADVISORY EDITOR
Richard C. Wade
PROFESSOR OF AMERICAN HISTORY
UNIVERSITY OF CHICAGO

MACHINE POLITICS AND MONEY IN ELECTIONS IN NEW YORK CITY

William Mills Ivins

ARNO PRESS
&
The New York Times
NEW YORK • 1970

Reprint Edition 1970 by Arno Press Inc.

Reprinted from a copy in The University of Illinois Library

LC# 71-112552
ISBN 0-405-02459-2

THE RISE OF URBAN AMERICA
ISBN for complete set 0-405-02430-4

Manufactured in the United States of America

No. 127   25 Cts.

Copyright, 1885,
by HARPER & BROTHERS
APRIL 15, 1887
Subscription Price
per Year, 52 Numbers, $15

Entered at the Post-Office at New York, as Second-class Mail Matter

MACHINE POLITICS

AND

MONEY IN ELECTIONS IN NEW YORK CITY

BY

WILLIAM M. IVINS

Copyright, 1887, by HARPER & BROTHERS

Books you may hold readily in your hand are the most useful, after all
DR. JOHNSON

NEW YORK
HARPER & BROTHERS, PUBLISHERS
1887

PUBLISHERS' ADVERTISEMENT.

No recent presentation of the abuses which have become part of the working of the political machinery of our great cities has attracted so much public attention as that made by Mr. Wm. M. Ivins, the City Chamberlain of New York. His address before the Commonwealth Club, with its supplementary papers, has formed the subject of newspaper discussion throughout the country, and has awakened an amount of interest in the reform of party methods of nomination and election which is well calculated to encourage those who have long regarded this reform as one of the most pressing necessities of our time. We have asked Mr. Ivins to place these papers at our disposal, with the view of satisfying a general desire to obtain them in a compact and collected form. With the addition of two of Mr. Ivins's articles, originally published in HARPER'S WEEKLY, the series will be found to constitute a work of exceptional value, possessing, as it does, the character of a treatise, at once exhaustive and thoroughly readable, on a subject of vital importance to the people of this city, and bearing with manifest directness on the conditions of pure politics in every part of the country. As an aid to the political education of young men, the book is no less valuable than as a guide to the promoters of reform legislation, and a contribution to the knowledge possessed by the great body of voters in regard to abuses which have done so much to obstruct the exercise of popular sovereignty. We have pleasure in accompanying this little volume with the assurance that its author possesses, in a very uncommon degree, the ability to discuss his subject with authority, clearness, and force, and we commend it very cordially to the attention of all patriotic citizens.

HARPER & BROTHERS.

FRANKLIN SQUARE, NEW YORK, *April* 4, 1887.

AUTHOR'S PREFACE.

THE papers here published were entirely occasional in their character. The first chapter was originally printed in the form of two articles in *Harper's Weekly* in the fall of 1884; the second and third chapters were part of a speech delivered at the February, 1887, dinner of the Commonwealth Club of New York. When asked to estimate the cost of an election in New York City, I found it necessary, in order to make the matter clear, to discuss not only our existing election law, but the relation of our party machinery to that law; and inasmuch as a knowledge of the constitution of the "Machine" is absolutely essential to an intelligent understanding of the motives and methods of the use of money in our elections, I have now thought it advisable to introduce the entire subject by the description of the "Machine" contained in the first chapter. The fourth and fifth chapters were called out by the general interest shown by the press and the public after the publication of the speech at the Commonwealth Club. They were contributed to the *New York Evening Post*, with the view of somewhat elaborating the points already touched upon, as well as of suggesting a remedy for the evils which I had already tried to describe. It has been suggested that in reprinting these papers I should also present a draft of a bill embodying the general suggestions contained in the English law, and adapting them to our own system of election machinery. After mature consideration, I have thought it better to leave such a draft-bill as I had prepared unpublished for the present. Furthermore, this course will have the effect of attracting all adverse criticism to the general plan, and not to any special details of a remedial measure. It is much better, at the present time, that the general outlines of the English system should be discussed than that criticism should be diverted to the consideration of minor details, such as the number of new officers to be appointed to distribute the ballots at each polling-place, the number of agents to be allowed to each candidate, the limit of permissible expenditure, etc. I am convinced that the fastening of attention on these subordinate and *variable* features would now be a mistake, for we are not yet near enough the time when it shall be necessary to determine upon them irrevocably. The bill when prepared should be the result of the most mature thought of the most experienced men, and one which will meet all possible objection other than such as may be fundamental and general. I therefore think it wiser not to propose a detailed measure until the debate has been completed, and yielded its full fruit of suggestion and criticism. I hold with Renan that "Time is the necessary collaborator of reason. The main point is to know how to wait."

I have added, in the form of an Appendix, a chapter on the actual results of the present English law as compared with those of a time antecedent to its enactment, which I hope will be found of interest to all students of the subject, although it is scarcely more than a compendium of newspaper articles.

I now offer the following pages to the public simply as documents *pour servir*, in the sincere hope that they may aid in the solution of the very difficult problem of democratic government in great cities.

W. M. I.

NEW YORK, *March*, 1887.

MACHINE POLITICS
AND
MONEY IN ELECTIONS
IN
NEW YORK CITY.

CHAPTER I.
THE MACHINE.

IT has been truly said that a citizen of New York generally knows little, if anything, more of the actual organization of political parties in this city than a Frenchman or an Englishman. The external working of party machinery is familiar, but the methods and motives which control the Machines are very little understood. The Machine may be organized nominally on the basis of Assembly Districts, as in Tammany Hall and the Republican party, or on that of Election Districts, as in the County Democracy; but there is really no difference between the two systems, the actual unit of organization always being the Assembly District. Of these latter there are in the city of New York twenty-four, which, in turn, are at present (1887) divided into eight hundred and twelve election districts, as will be shown more in detail hereafter. The Machine is governed directly from the centre, and is a close corporation. The Assembly District organizations receive their policy, even in matters purely local, from the central authority, although this is not so uniformly the rule in the Republican as in the Democratic party.

Nominally all power ultimately falls into the hands of a caucus of the leaders of the twenty-four Assembly Districts, but it actually rests with one or perhaps half a dozen individuals in this interior cabal, who are absolute. This one or these few are men who hold prominent offices, or who have independent means and are ambitious for control. The former of these two classes supply offices for their subordinates and followers, and the latter class contribute out of their personal means for campaign purposes. In conference— which is a formality always strictly adhered to— these leaders can invariably compel adherence to their views by at least a majority of the caucus, and thus through the formal government of the majority give the semblance of democratic methods to the course pursued. In these caucuses the inquiry is not what the district leaders or the people of the districts really think best, but what the few men in control have decided upon. So true is this that there are few men of practical experience in politics who have not at times heard as serious complaints from the captains of tens and of hundreds because of their inability to find out exactly what is expected of them, as because they are deprived of a voice in framing the policy of the party.

A single department is of itself enough to furnish the foundations of a Machine. It only requires that the department be one in which there are a score of fair places for superior politicians, and a laborers' pay-roll for the rank and file. A great department like that of the Public Works can, when in the hands of a politician, always be controlled for the maintenance of a powerful organization which shall for all practical purposes be the personal property of the departmental head. The better offices are distributed among those who are expected to fill the position of district leaders;

or if, as is frequently the case, some man who has a passion for politics, but who does not care for an office, assumes the leadership of a district, one of the better offices is given to such person as he shall select, who becomes the district lieutenant. These leaders and lieutenants are expected, in conformity with the tacitly understood terms of their contract, to obey the central power uncomplainingly, and to devote so much of their days, nights, and salaries as may be necessary to keep their districts properly organized, and as much of the remnant of their time as they conveniently can to the service of the city. The offices thus come to be regarded by professionals simply as a means of supplying a livelihood to those who are willing to devote themselves to politics and the service of their leaders. In other words, the offices only too frequently are used merely as a means of paying politicians for pursuing their profession in the service of a party or of a particular individual. And while a majority of the leaders and subordinates who hold office perform sufficiently faithful service to the city, but a small minority escape the detailed duties of the Machine in addition to those which they render the public officially. The capital of the Machines thus consists of the nine thousand nine hundred and fifty-five subordinate places on the pay-rolls; this number does not include the Congressmen, Senators, Assemblymen, Aldermen, and eighty-three important officers, such as heads of city departments or bureaus, nor does it include any subordinate employés of the state or national Government whatever.

The duties of an Assembly District leader are manifold. If he wishes a strong following in his district he must be at the service day and night of his neighbors, who, in return for the services rendered them, are willing to attend primaries or vote at elections. A young man is arrested for fast driving: the district leader must visit a police justice and intercede for him. An old man wants to keep an apple-stand on a frequented corner: the district leader must see his Alderman and have a special ordinance passed over the Mayor's veto. A city ordinance has been violated, and the violator reported by the police to the Corporation Attorney: the district leader must see the Corporation Attorney and have the complaint pigeon-holed; or, if he fail in this, he must see the justice and have it dismissed when it is called for trial. If a laborer who can serve him is out of work, he must find something for him to do on the streets, or on the aqueduct, or in the parks. If a builder employing a number of men, or a lot-owner who is putting up a house, wants four or five feet of the city's property, free of cost, on which to build a "swell front" or a bay-window, the leader must see that the application runs through the board, with or without the Mayor's consent. If a corporation wants to dig a vault under the street to its very centre, he must lend a hand to put the matter through. If a liquor dealer is arrested for selling without a license, he must leave no stone unturned to secure his escape unpunished. Finally, if a poor devil is in want of a dollar, he must let him have it. He must attend all political meetings, go to club picnics, attend church fairs, not permit himself to be forgotten in the liquor stores and other places of frequent resort, and must hold himself generally in readiness to do whatever is required of him by the superior chiefs.

He needs a number of captains, and if any respect be paid to the plan of organization on the basis of election districts, he should have one in each of these minor divisions. Each of these captains has some sort of place for himself, or his son, or his nephew, and has some sort of control over the voters of two or three thickly populated houses. If he is enterprising, he buys a horse and cart and hires a driver, and then has them employed in the service of the city, in street repairs, in removing ashes and sweepings, or in sprinkling the streets. If he is enabled to put two or three carts to work, he is peculiarly fortunate, is sure of an income, can enjoy his leisure, and devote himself to demonstrating the honesty, capacity, and superior democracy or republicanism of his employers, besides doing all manner of neighborly offices for those who may need them. He obeys his Assembly District leader, whoever he may be, respecting the office rather than the man. Whenever the central caucus or the boss desires it, they can reorganize the district, and select a new leader, to whom all the captains must report, or surrender their livings. They consequently succumb, and give the most perfect demonstration of the "cohesive power of public plunder," or, as Demosthenes called it, the "cement of office." There is no patronage, however, that a district leader desires so much and seeks so eagerly as places on the police force. As a patrolman his friend can, in an unobtrusive and quiet way, render him and the party valuable service. A roundsman is more desirable still, while a sergeant or captain is a real power if he takes any interest in politics—and some of them do.

It is in this connection that the Civil Service laws are destined to play havoc with the Machine, because, although removals for disobedience of political orders can still be made, the places cannot be disposed of to new men. The most thoroughgoing Machine politician, if Commissioner of Public Works or of Street Cleaning, could no longer make either of those departments the *cadre* of a political organization in the good old-fashioned way, for all appointments other than of laborers and heads of bureaus have now to be made from lists submitted by the Civil Service examiners. Consequently it is now better for a commissioner, if a politician, to overlook political disobedience, if not too grave, than to create a vacancy, and run the risk of losing the political value of the place altogether through the possible necessity for appointing some qualified veteran of the war, some person of opposite political faith, or some graduate from a counting-house, who may have taken a

THE MACHINE.   15

high mark in the competitive examinations. The politicians, always fertile in expedients, are continually inventing ways to evade the spirit of these laws, but it will not be long before their resources for evasion shall be exhausted and all possible contingencies fully provided for by the regulations and schedules.

In this way a compact body of men is always in existence for party purposes. First, there are the bosses, sachems, commissioners, or what not; then the Assembly District leaders; then eight hundred or more minor lieutenants or election district captains for each organization, each of whom can command the services, in return for those rendered by themselves, of from five to ten voters. The figures thus run up into thousands, and the organization not only being compact, but reaching into every district, the material exists for large and enthusiastic mass-meetings, for well-attended primaries, for an active canvass throughout the city, and, above all, for a thorough manning of the polls on election day. The internal organization of parties is such that independent and thoughtful voters can take part in preliminary party activity only as counters in a game played by professionals, or at the cost of seeing every effort at independent activity nullified by the power of the Machine. Sometimes this nullification is effected by a suborned majority, sometimes by physical violence, and sometimes through outright fraud and the falsification of the records. If this be objected to, and an appeal be taken to the central body, a hearing may be accorded, but there is no record of a case in which such an appeal has ever been determined against the district leader, or the man whom the "bosses" had prearranged should be assisted to supplant the district leader.

The Machine organization, then, takes some such form as this: A County Committee, consisting of so many members from each of the several Assembly Districts, who in their several localities make up the Assembly District committees; an executive committee of the County Committee, made up of the leaders of each Assembly District and a few of their most influential lieutenants and friends; a sub-committee of this executive committee, consisting of the Assembly District leaders, about twenty-four in number, who in their turn are governed by those who employ them for political service and pay them out of the public fund. The boss consults with the leaders, and does what they wish if it accords with his views; otherwise the leaders do what the boss wishes. Then they call the Executive Committee together in order that it may act spontaneously in the premises, which it generally does in such a way as to prove conclusively the unanimity of purpose in that body. The necessary resolutions are then passed for submission by way of report to the General Committee of the county, by whom they are uniformly carried, thus expressing the single will of that body.

At first sight it would appear that a body of two thousand or more men could not be easily handled, and neither could it be if each one had individual views; but the politicians well know that, with such organizations as theirs, a large body is much more easily managed than a small one. Each district leader is expected to, and does, answer for his district contingent, and in the city of New York, consequently, it only needs that thirteen out of the twenty-four leaders should be agreed for these thirteen to carry committee or convention, since they are really and directly responsible for all of the representatives from their districts. This rule works particularly well in the case of certain conventions, like the County Convention, where there are always two thousand or more delegates, and which Convention is practically the General Committee under another name. The twenty-four leaders first having agreed with the boss upon a ticket, the Convention is called together, and the twenty-four (who are always members of the Convention), through their subordinates, confirm the work as agreed upon. If any one objects he is laughed at; perhaps he is heard, but no harm is done, and the vote will stand anywhere from unanimity to two thousand against ten or a hundred.

By such a Machine the politicians really control the city, for they know that the very laws conspire in their favor. The politicians begin by making it impossible for any man who earns his living outside of politics to keep up with them, and then the law steps in and calls for the election of so many persons that it is practically impossible for the voter to learn anything about the candidates, or to wisely determine for whom he should vote, much less to put any one in nomination with the hope of election. He usually falls back upon his party nominee, and so the Machine is justified and kept in power by the votes

THE MACHINE. 19

of the very people whom it has practically deprived of political equality. In this way leaders who do not get appointive offices are elected to the Board of Aldermen, the Senate, the Assembly, or to a civil justiceship, as the case may be. Thus the vicious circle is completed.

The politicians and many of the newspapers alike say that the remedy is for the people to attend the primaries. Now of these latter there are three classes: the Republican, where the voting is done by Assembly Districts and from the rolls of the district organization; the Tammany, where it is done by Assembly Districts, and where every one whom the inspectors permit may vote; and the County Democracy, where it is done by election districts and from the registry lists. In the case of the Republican primaries the elections are controlled by committees on Revision of Rolls, by shortening the hours for voting, by loading the line, and by the inspectors who make the returns. In the case of Tammany there is nothing to be done except formally to register the will of the leader, and what is called the primary is usually only a gathering of the clans to get a drink, and incidentally vote the ticket put into their hands.

In the case of the County Democracy there is a greater show of fairness at the polls in election districts, but one can never tell who has been elected in case of a contest until the matter has been submitted to a committee on contested seats, and then the overwhelming strength and startling regularity of the leader's friends are always demonstrated. A point of the utmost consequence is the determination of the place at which the primary is to be held, and the place being named by the district leader, the voting is usually done at that liquor store, cigar store, livery-stable, or other place where the contestant favored by the leader can best control the house, its exits and entrances, and can most easily and speedily gather his voters together. As a consequence, nothing is more eagerly sought for, where it is apparent that there is to be a closely contested primary, than the determination of the place for holding it.

The following very instructive table has been prepared by Mr. Robert Graham, of New York, showing how many of the primary and convention meetings held immediately preceding the election of 1884 were held in liquor saloons or next door to them :*

---

* See Appendix I.

THE MACHINE. 21

	LIQUOR SALOONS.					NEXT DOOR TO SALOONS.					NEITHER.				
	Tammany Hall.	Irving Hall.	County Democracy.	Republican.	Total.	Tammany Hall.	Irving Hall.	County Democracy.	Republican.	Total.	Tammany Hall.	Irving Hall.	County Democracy.	Republican.	Total.
Congressional Convention.	6	7	6	.	19	.	1	.	.	1	3	.	3	.	6
Assembly Convention....	17	18	19	9	63	.	3	1	3	7	7	3	4	12	26
Aldermanic Convention...	17	19	19	9	64	.	3	1	3	7	7	2	4	12	25
Primaries..........	16	19	443	9	487	.	3	65	3	71	8	2	204	12	226
Totals.....	56	63	487	27	633	.	10	67	9	86	25	7	215	36	283

Political Meetings held in Saloon............ 633
Political Meetings held next door to Saloon.... 86
                                              ─────
                                              719
Political Meetings held apart from Saloons... 283
                                              ─────
Total.................. 1,002

The apparent disproportion between the County Democracy and the other organizations in the use of liquor saloons is due to the fact that the former has at least eight hundred and twelve primaries, one for each election district, while the latter have only twenty-four each, or one for each Assembly District. Where eight hundred and twelve primaries are to be held the number of voters to be accommodated at each is naturally small, and inexpensive places have to be found. To the local politician the public-house thus presents superior attractions from whatever point of view it may be regarded.

Chief among all the benefits accruing to the party through such an organization as has been described is the control of the election booths and ballots. According to long-established custom, each party must have a ticket booth for each polling-place in the city, attached to which booth there are a number of paid ticket peddlers, who receive five dollars each on the average for their day's work at the polls. All tickets, folded, bunched, and bagged, are originally distributed from headquarters to the twenty-four Assembly District leaders, and they in their turn carry the distribution down into election districts. This enables them to control the situation so far as their localities are concerned, for they can unbunch any candidate they like, and bunch any other they wish, and there are districts in which all the chances are in favor of the bunch being voted as made up. In their turn the election district peddlers at the polls can do the same thing in a small way upon the day of election, and cut and trade as they prefer or as they are directed. Upon occasion this sort of business is done by the bosses themselves, as in the Mayoral election of 1882, when the Republican machinists sent out from headquarters the tickets of the Tammany candidate for Mayor in place of those of their own nominee. There are some districts in the city where this ability to handle the tickets has been worth a year's income to the local leaders.

These are but a few of the details of political organization in the city of New York, and the statements, necessarily general, are every one of them susceptible of rich illustration. It is no wonder that honest citizens can never get control of the Machine from within, and can rarely successfully fight it from without, for in either event they must devote so much time to it that they have not enough left to earn a living. The Machine is governed by a singleness of purpose, which produces a compactness against which good citizens can only break themselves to pieces when fighting it from within, while if they organize an outside opposition in which everything is done by honest discussion, compactness is almost impossible of achievement. The single matter of properly manning the polls requires the action of at least several thousand picked and loyal men, who should stand at the booths from principle and not for money, and to be sure of such a body requires little less than a revolution in public feeling. Those who do this work for their parties are either office-holders or paid peddlers, and in either case are only earning their living. The politicians would not be difficult to beat if the people would organize for their own protection and from principle; but it is the matter of organization which is difficult, and no one understands this better than the bosses.

But the Machines have other immense advantages. Not only does our army of policemen contribute to the election expenses of the several Machines, but they have it within their power to become the mightiest of electioneering agents, and to compel great classes into voting as they wish. In this respect, and notably when in Republican hands, the District Attorney's office has sometimes been a very powerful political engine. It has never been very difficult to tell how the liquor dealers, gamblers, dance-house keepers, and the drunken and disorderly generally would vote: like other people, they are very careful to look out for number one. The community thought that the law entitling them to watchers at the canvass of the vote after the close of the polls would secure them an honest count, but the Board of Police appoint the canvassers and poll-clerks whom the machinists select, and the intelligent and ingenious policeman, if a partisan, need never long want an excuse for ejecting the official watchers from the room, as more than one reputable but misguided man who has volunteered to serve as such can testify.

The Machine suffices for all things, even for the support of a powerful newspaper organ. Nothing could excel the simplicity of the device by which a certain daily paper in this city was at a critical time kept alive as a distributor of news, as a defender of the " bosses," and at the same time made self-supporting, and even enabled to pay a dividend on its stock, the majority of which was held by those very bosses. There are a good many liquor dealers in New York; they are numbered by thousands, and are all required to have licenses. These licenses are given by the Board of Excise. This board, being agreed on party policy, had only to demand of every liquor dealer the production of his receipt for one or more subscriptions to the daily organ before granting a license, and the circulation of the paper was assured, and in those very places, the liquor stores and political exchanges, where it would do most good. And this is no fanciful case, but matter of party history.

The Machine finds but little difficulty in raising the necessary funds to defray its expenses. This is particularly the case with the majority Machines, whose nominations are equivalent to elections. They can collect largely from actual office-holders, and can practically put up the offices at auction to the highest, bidder, and impose such assessments as they see fit. If the natural expenses of a campaign are heavy, so much the better for the Machine, and so much the worse for the people. The Machine can raise the money; the advocates of an independent and honest movement cannot. And yet in the long-run the people pay these expenses. They are unwilling to contribute to secure good government, but in effect they contribute to perpetuate the bad; for those who pay the assessments to run the Machine get the money from the people by way of salaries, and eventually it all comes into the tax budget. But the average ratepayer is politically torpid, or timid and shortsighted.

It will be seen from this survey, as well as from what is to follow, that the Machine is built up on the spoils of place, and the necessity for voluntary provision by the electors of an extra-legal election machinery.

CHAPTER II.

THE ELECTION LAWS.

IN endeavoring to eliminate from the mass of rumor and general indefinite knowledge definite facts, as nearly as they are ascertainable, concerning the expenditure of money in elections, whether paid out of the public treasury or by individuals, and the manner of its collection and disbursement, it is necessary, after knowing something of the organization of the Machine, to understand the election laws. That the facts are such as to demonstrate the existence of a great evil, we all know in a rough-and-ready way. How great that evil is, and exactly how it affects and modifies the purposes for which the law invests us all with the elective franchise, can only be known, however, when the facts are laid before us with something of the exactness and definiteness of a financial statement; and while, to my mind, there is no question of the day of greater importance than

THE ELECTION LAWS. 29

this, there is none concerning which accurate data are more difficult of ascertainment. The figures given in the newspapers or talked of at the clubs are rarely to be relied upon, although sometimes approximately correct. The men who raise and the men who expend the money, as a rule, keep their knowledge to themselves; and one not in the secret is rarely if ever able to discover the amount of money spent at an election by parties as parties, or by the individual candidates as such. The very secretness of the ways in which the money is raised and disbursed renders the correct figures almost impossible of access. Nevertheless, it is necessary to get at them, not vaguely but accurately, if our work is to be more valuable than a lot of useless guesses or unreliable gossip.

In this regard we are in exactly the same position to-day that England was in prior to the passage of the Prevention of Corrupt Practices Act. There the public was regarded as being so plainly and clearly entitled to this knowledge that the amount of permissible expenditure by candidates is limited by law, and the candidate compelled to make a sworn statement of the amount expended. Here, however, we have no such aid to the discovery of the facts. Under our system it is impossible for any one to get at and understand the details of election expenditure without a really thorough and accurate knowledge of our election machinery and our election laws. Not only is the present expenditure in and about elections almost directly attributable to the insufficiency of our election laws, but our political Machines, with all their worst evils, are the result of that insufficiency far more than of any inherent tendency to corruption. So long as the Election Law remains as it is to-day, party machinery will be dominant, corruption will be rife, the primary will be a farce, and the legislative recognition of parties, party machinery, and party primaries will only intensify the evils.

The general theory of our law is that it takes no notice of parties. Until very recently it did not recognize their existence at all. The point of view of the law was that every man is entitled to vote as he pleases; to name his own candidate, cast his own ballot, and, in a word, in the matter of the franchise to act with perfect independence. The original theory was that any voter might write the name of any person whomsoever upon any piece of paper, take it to the polls, and cast it

THE ELECTION LAWS. 31

as his ballot; that the law knew no difference between men or between parties, and that all men being equal, if some saw fit to act together as an organized party, they were entirely in their right in so doing. From the very beginning, however, the independent voters were the stragglers, and parties practically controlled nominations, and one or the other of the party nominees was almost invariably elected. The first expenditure in and about elections, therefore, was that incident to securing the control of delegates to conventions and leaders of caucuses; the second, that to secure the election at the polls.

Under our early system the Election Law simply called for the selection of sworn inspectors. The inspector was supposed to know every voter who came to the polls, either of his own knowledge or by the assistance of the neighbors of the voter; and every one who came to the polls was permitted to cast his ballot with no other impediment than that of swearing it in in case he was challenged. It is not necessary to discuss the gradual evolution of the present Election Law in our great cities. The simple primitive system practically held good in this city until the times of

William M. Tweed. Then it became necessary to limit by legislation the almost complete and perfect freedom of individual action in and about elections, in order to prevent frauds as great as that which in this State resulted in the counting out of one Governor who was elected and counting in of another who was not elected, as is generally believed to have been done in 1868. No measure ever proposed by the Legislature of this State really met with more opposition than the original Registration Act for the city of New York. It was decried as undemocratic; and had it not been for the absolute necessity for some such prevention of criminality at elections, it could not have been passed.

This law provided for the registration and identification of all voters. It was the parent of our present system, which must be summarized in order to bring out clearly and perfectly the relation between it and the political machinery of our different municipal parties.

At the election in this city the ballot-boxes used for receiving the ballots are marked and numbered successively from one to eight, and are supplied at the public expense. The manner of printing, folding, and indorsing the ballots, as well as their size, shape, and the quality of paper used, is generally prescribed by law. The polling-places are open at six o'clock in the morning, and close at four o'clock in the afternoon. The election and canvass of the votes is to be conducted in conformity with the general election laws of the State, except as they are modified by special legislation affecting the city itself. The Board of Police is required to establish a Bureau of Elections, the force of which bureau are subject to such rules, regulations, and orders as the Board of Police may from time to time adopt; and it is conducted by a single person, to be selected by the Board of Police, whose term of office is three years, and whose salary is fixed by the Police Board, but which may not exceed $5000 a year. It is the duty of the Board of Police to cause books to be prepared for the registry of names and facts required by law; the form of these registers is prescribed by statute. The Board of Police is authorized to divide the city into election districts. Each election district is to contain, as nearly as practicable, two hundred and fifty voters on the basis of the registration. Under the present law the Board of Police may in every even year divide such election districts as by the registration of the two preceding years shall be found to have an average of over four hundred voters. It is the duty of the chief of the Bureau of Elections to preserve the records of the Police Board pertaining to the conduct of the affairs of his bureau, prepare and furnish all necessary registers, books, maps, forms, oaths, certificates, blanks, and instructions for the use of the inspectors of the election, and to have the custody of and keep all records and papers. He appoints a chief clerk, and the Board of Police furnish him with such other clerical force among the patrolmen in the Department as he may from time to time need. All inspectors of elections and poll-clerks in the city are selected and appointed by the Board of Police, who have power to make all necessary removals and transfers, and fill all vacancies. They are called upon to appoint four inspectors in each district; and in a provision of the law vesting them with this power we find a most curious recognition of the existence of two parties, and only two, which section of the statute reads as follows:

"It shall be the duty of the said Board of Police annually, in the months of August and September in each succeeding year, in each election district of said city or county, to select to serve as inspectors of election four persons, two of whom on State issues shall be of different faith and opinion from their associates, and those appointed to represent the party and political minority on State issues in the said city and county, to be named solely by such of the Commissioners of the Police in the Police Board as are the representatives of such political minority."

These inspectors are required to be citizens of good character, able to read, write, and speak the English language, qualified voters of the city and county, and not candidates for any office to be voted for by the electors of the district for which they shall be selected; but no person is required to be a resident of the election district for which he shall be appointed an inspector. After nomination and approval they are sworn into office, the term of which is one year, unless they are sooner removed for want of the requisite qualifications.

Two persons of different political faith and opinions on State issues, and possessing the same qualifications as those required for inspectors, are required to be in all respects similarly selected and appointed as poll-clerks for each election district, their term of office being also for one year. The law provides for the compensation of these inspectors and poll-clerks at the rate of $7.50 per day for each day's service at any registration or election, which compensation is paid on the certificate of the chief of the Bureau of Elections.

The inspectors are vested with power to preserve order at the place of registration and at the polls on election-day, to suppress riot, protect voters and challengers, and to appoint electors to assist them in so doing. There are four registration days prior to election. The registers are made in triplicate, and prior to election are published in full in the *City Record*.

At the close of the poll the vote is canvassed by the inspectors of election in public and without adjournment, until it is completed, and no canvass can be made unless at least six persons, if so many claim that privilege, are allowed to be present and so near that they can see whether the duties of the inspector are faithfully performed; each candidate

THE ELECTION LAWS.

for an office to be filled at an election is permitted to designate by certificate in writing, signed by him, one person in each election district for which he is a candidate to be present at the canvass of the ballots for that office, and this witness is entitled to the protection prescribed by the law.

The statute is long, intricate, and complex, consisting of ninety-two sections, the last but one of which provides that the legal compensation of all inspectors of election, and poll-clerks, and other officers of election, the cost and expenses of all necessary election notices, posters, maps, advertisements, registers, books, blanks, and stationery, the rent and cost of fitting up, warming, lighting, cleaning, and safe-keeping of the places of registration, of furnishing, repairing, and carting ballot-boxes, and of all supplies of every kind and nature for all elections in the city of New York, shall be a city charge.

This statute has been taken as a model in many States, and it certainly does almost entirely prevent the evils from which we suffered so long, that is, open frauds at elections in the casting and counting of the ballots. But the occasion which gave rise to the statute also dictated the limitations of its application. It has reference only to so much of the machinery of election as refers to the registration, taking and canvassing of the vote; and although it prescribes the form in which tickets are to be printed, the number of tickets, the manner of folding and indorsing, it is entirely silent upon the vital point as to how the tickets are to be distributed.

Now this very point is the pivotal one around which the entire political machinery of this city revolves, whether that machinery be Democratic or Republican. It exists for only one purpose, the securing of the vote on election-day, and it is organized accordingly. In its organization it actually makes the Election Law not only an adjunct to the Machine, but treats the election officers as so many men in the pay of the city, whom it can count upon to cast their ballots as the party desires, and to keep a close scrutiny upon all voters whatever, from a partisan as well as an official point of view.*

---

* See Appendix II.

CHAPTER III.

THE COST OF ELECTIONS IN NEW YORK CITY.

IN discussing the cost of elections, we must begin with the election machinery itself. In the city of New York there are to-day 812 election districts. The law provides for four inspectors and two poll-clerks to each district, making an aggregate of 4872 election officers paid out of the City Treasury; 2436 of which are Democrats, and 2436 of which are Republicans. The Republican Police Commissioners appoint the Republican election officers; the Democratic Police Commissioners those who are Democratic.

The Democratic party, however, is divided into a number of factions, and the Democratic members of the Board of Police have for years required that the representation of the factions should be in proportion to their recognition as to regularity by the Democratic State Committee.

In this way Tammany Hall Democrats have had two-fifths of one-half, the County Democrats two-fifths of one-half, and Irving Hall one-fifth of one half of the election officers.

This system, sanctioned by the statute and the Supreme Court, consequently enables the Republicans to supply places to three men for each election district in the city for five days each at $7.50 apiece a day, and the Democrats do the same thing in the ratio of division which has been mentioned. The total appropriation for all election purposes whatever in the city of New York last year (1886), made under the provisions of the Election Law, was $226,000.

It is customary for the designation of the polling-places also to be treated as patronage, but it is not bestowed directly on the political parties as in the case of inspectors and poll-clerks. It is police captains' patronage. Under instructions of the chief of the Bureau of Elections— who was for many years, if he is not yet, a party "boss"—the Superintendent of Police each year asks the captains to recommend one place in each election district in their respective precincts to be rented as a polling-place. The owner of a butcher's, baker's, barber's, or tobacconist's shop regards the designation of his place as a valuable favor, and the allotment is much sought after in the several election districts. It is not only a good advertisement, but the lessor of the premises is well paid for advertising his business in this way. The eight hundred and twelve places are accordingly selected by the police captains, and the majority being Republicans, the greater part of this patronage is awarded to Republicans of good party standing.

The appropriation to the Police Board by the Board of Estimate and Apportionment for last year was made in detail as follows:

For compensation of inspectors and poll-clerks (section 1854, New York City Consolidation Act of 1882).............................	$145,480
For rent of polling-places and fitting up the same, new ballot-boxes, carting ballot-boxes, stationery, maps, and printing, etc...........	40,720
For advertising election districts, polling-places, and the official canvass, for advertising election notices by Clerk of Common Council, for advertising election notices by the Sheriff, and for serving supervisors with notices of elections by the Sheriff...................	25,000
For expenses of special election in Sixth Assembly District on December 29, 1885......	2,800

For compensation of clerks to Board of Canvassers................................	$2,000	
For salary of the chief of the Bureau of Elections....................................	5,000	$216,000
For salary of the Chief Clerk of the Bureau of Elections...............................	1,500	
		6,500
		$222,500

By subsequent transfer $3500 was added, making the total as given at page 40 of $226,000.

In addition to this patronage growing out of the express provisions of the State law, there is a large volume of patronage of much the same character rising out of the application of the United States law to elections in those years when United States officers are chosen, or say every other year. The national law calls for the appointment of two supervisors of election for each election district, who are to be paid $5 per day for not over ten days' service. They are appointed by a judge of the United States Court. During the last election the supervisors served from one to seven days each. The Treasury Department has decided, whether rightfully or wrongfully, that none of them can be paid for more than five days' service. Assuming that they be paid for an average of five

COST OF ELECTIONS IN NEW YORK CITY. 43

days' service only, we have $25 for each supervisor, two supervisors for each district, or say $50 per election district for eight hundred and twelve election districts, or $40,600.

In addition to the supervisors, the United States Marshal is authorized to appoint on the application of two citizens in writing as many deputy marshals as he pleases. During the last election the United States Marshal appointed but two marshals from each district, and limited their term of office to two days each, at $5 per day. This is the smallest expenditure that has ever been made in this respect since the enactment of the law under which the assistant marshals are appointed, the Republicans having invariably appointed a larger number to serve for a greater length of time.

In addition to this, the United States Marshal appointed a general aid for ten days at $5 per day, and three Assembly District marshals for each district at $5 per day for six days each; he also appointed three marshals-at-large for ten days each. He advises me that his printing bill for blanks for applications, appointments, instructions, etc., was $1500, and his payments to marshals $22,000, which, with the payment to supervisors of $40,600, makes an actual total for last year of $64,100 for this purpose. These places have heretofore always been treated as party patronage, and the money has been distributed accordingly.

The legal machinery of elections thus involves the expenditure of $290,000 as a minimum, paid out of the public purse and treated as party patronage, which expenditure in Presidential elections of the past has been greater than this by fully $200,000, incident to the immense number of appointments made by the United States Marshal, and the special work done by the Chief Supervisor of Elections. I have not had the time at my disposal to get the exact figures for any but last year, however, and these latter I give on official authority. This fund of $290,000 is practically used, if not to purchase, at least to assure and guarantee the vote of at least ten persons for each election district. The election districts will average about 300 voters, so that 3 per cent. of the voters are employed in or about the elections in accordance with the provisions of law as officers of the law, and the election district leader sees that they are the first men to vote, and to vote right.

The inspectors, poll-clerks, supervisors, and marshals are generally selected for the same reasons, and in the same way in which the workers at the polls are chosen. It was customary during the entire time the Republicans had control of the appointment of the supervisors and marshals for them to distribute a certain number of blanks among the district leaders of the Republican party and of Tammany Hall, to be filled up with such names as the Assembly District leader should choose; the men so chosen were appointed if their character was not flagrantly bad, and many times during the earlier administration of the law their character was not looked to at all. As to the inspectors and poll-clerks, it is customary for each organization, knowing exactly how many men it should get, to divide the number up among the Assembly Districts, and permit each Assembly District leader to name his representatives. This is an element of personal strength to the leader, and a guarantee of the political soundness, both as to general faith and fidelity to the organization, of the person appointed.

Now, as has been pointed out, the entire political machinery of New York City is incident to the main fact of getting in the votes on election-day. Every part of the Machine is organized with this object in view and no other.

There are three well-organized Machines in New York City. Each of these Machines, it will be remembered, has twenty-four district organizations, corresponding with the Assembly Districts of the city. Each Assembly District organization consists of a committee varying in numbers according to the general plan of organization. Ultimately and essentially, however, all the organizations are alike; each Assembly District is actually controlled by the Assembly District leader, and the caucus of the Assembly District leaders constitutes the main-spring of the party. It is the source of all authority, and determines all questions of policy. Each of the parties asserts that its policy is dictated either by its Conventions or by its County Committee; but, in fact, the delegates to the Conventions or to the County Committee from each Assembly District consist of only such persons as are satisfactory to the district leader. The district leader himself is, as a rule, chosen either by the boss of the party or by a vote of the majority of the other district leaders,

COST OF ELECTIONS IN NEW YORK CITY. 47

except in those cases where they have compelled their recognition by the strength of their personal following in the district. Committees of the organization have the power of passing upon the validity or invalidity of all primary and committee elections, and, as a rule, decide all contests as the recognized district leader desires. For the purpose of showing the best results in his district, it is customary for each district leader to have a representative to look after the election district, commonly called an election district captain. These men are of the utmost importance to the Machine, and every Assembly District leader strives to quarter his election district captains on the city. This he succeeds in doing sooner or later. If the Republicans are out of power in every other department, and cannot take care of the "boys" in any other way, they at least always have three places to dispose of, which are worth $7.50 a day for five days in each election district; but they are not reduced to this sore necessity. The Democratic leader either finds a place for the friends of the Republican leader, with whom he is co-operating, or when the Republican leader is in power it is the latter who finds places for his Democratic friends and coadjutors; for the professional or caste feeling is very strong, and the politicians of all parties recognize their ultimate community of interests at all times. Sooner or later, on the pay-rolls of the city, which contain 9955 names, exclusive of school-rolls, or 13,749 all told, which latter figure includes 25 Aldermen and 83 chief officers, and excludes all Assemblymen, Senators, and national officers, at least four men are taken care of by each party all the year round in each of the eight hundred and twelve districts. The Machine, for the purpose of securing their services in perpetuity, thus has the city pay them as city employés. This is particularly the case with regard to the Assembly District leaders. To be sure, the money paid them out of the city, state, or national Treasury cannot properly be said to be money spent in elections, but it is money spent in maintaining the solidity and perpetuity of the Machine; it keeps it alive the year round, and ready for all emergencies, and especially for the great critical emergency of the election. Without it each election would find the Machine broken and scattered, and consequently it has to be considered.

New York City paid its Assembly District leaders last year $330,000, or an average of $4750 for each of the seventy-two leaders. This figure includes the estimated income of the Register's office at $100,000. That is now, however, a salaried office, yielding only $12,000 per year to its chief. The amount which is now being actually received by these leaders from the public treasury is $242,000. Of this amount Tammany Hall gets about $119,000, divided among eighteen out of twenty-four of its district leaders. The County Democracy gets about $90,000, divided among seventeen out of twenty-five of its district leaders. The Republican leaders, being in the minority party, both in the city and nation, do not fare so well; but they have hopes, or have heretofore shared the pay of loyalty. Their $32,000 is divided among eight of their twenty-four leaders. It must be said, however, in order to be just, that many of the men among whom these sums are divided are honest and efficient public servants, and the city gets full value for the salaries paid them.

The aggregate of these sums, say $242,000, may be regarded as the city's permanent investment in the machines for leadership alone. Certainly not less than $1,000,000 more is invested in the same way in political captains and followers, of whom it must be said, also, that the great majority render fair service to the city for the salaries paid them. The Machines thus supported all the year round find themselves in good condition to take up the work of organizing a campaign and conducting an election.

When our County Clerk and Register were respectively feed officers, they were frequently called upon, not only to pay a very high assessment, but to support a certain number of district leaders, thus giving these leaders their liberty throughout the entire year, which they were consequently enabled to devote to the interests of their party and constituencies; $15,000 to $50,000 has not been regarded as too large an assessment to pay for these offices. It is an open secret among politicians that for a number of years three or four people had from $3000 to $5000 apiece per annum from each of these offices, who rendered no official service whatever, and who, nevertheless, were quartered upon the Sheriff, Register, and the County Clerk, as only a fair distribution of the income from these offices to the Machine which presented them to their holders.

COST OF ELECTIONS IN NEW YORK CITY. 51

Prior to election-day each party formally, through the action of its leaders in caucus, determines upon how much money shall be allotted by the party, as such, for expenditure in each election district, to employ workers at the polls, as it is called. These workers at the polls are paid an average of five dollars a day each. The ballots are printed by each Machine for itself, although frequently they all employ the same printer, which has sometimes in the past produced strange results. It is usual to select a committee on printing, which takes charge of the entire matter of getting up the ballot, seeing that it conforms with the requirements of the law, and that it is folded, bunched, and distributed throughout the organization.

The manner of distribution is as follows: The printer bunches the tickets into complete sets. He then puts, we will say, from two thousand five hundred to five thousand sets in an election district bag, and then puts one of these bags for each election district into a larger bag, which is marked with the number of the Assembly District to which it is to go. In Tammany Hall and the County Democracy, on the night before the election, the distribution of these bags is supervised by the

Committee of the organization, the Assembly District bag being given to the Assembly District leader; he in his turn calls together the election district leaders, and places in the hands of each of them the election district bag. In the Republican party, however, all tickets are delivered flat, as printed, to the district leaders, who supervise the folding and bunching, which is done by the leaders, each for his own district. This is a right the Republican leaders have never been willing to surrender, as it would materially depreciate the value of their franchise as leaders. As leaders of the minority party, and often holding the balance of power, this is of great political or cash value to them, and cannot be given up to the control of the central organization any more than any other valuable proprietary right.

The Assembly District leaders thus come into possession of the whole of the vital part of the election machinery. They could meet on the night before election and destroy the tickets, and no election could take place. It is the possession of this power which makes them valuable from the point of view of purchase and sale. Many of the Assembly District leaders in the three organizations have exploited this power so successfully and profitably that they have been able to live throughout the entire year on their income derived from the handling of the tickets. They can destroy, rebunch, fail to distribute, and what not, as they please, and thus give rise to such controversies as that between **Mr. Thorndike Rice** and **Mr. Michael Cregan**, in which the whole community was lately interested. They rarely, if ever, take money nominally for dealing with the tickets. It is taken, or alleged to be taken, for the purpose of securing the distribution or peddling of the tickets at the polls, or, as it is called, for the "employment of workers."

The result of this system of machinery is that, in order to compete with the professional politicians, it is necessary for any independent body of citizens to have a very complex Machine, and frequently a very expensive one. In the first place, the regular Machine is always equipped and prepared to print as well as to distribute a ticket. These are expensive matters, and the fact of the expense in this regard alone is a practical deterrent to independent movements for reform. The Machines are always enabled to print the tickets and distribute them by means of assessments levied on candidates and office-holders.

First as to assessments—and these assessments, be it understood, are something entirely distinct and apart from the amount of moneys paid voluntarily by candidates in the prosecution of their canvass independent of or accessary to the work of the Machine. In good years, such as that after the sale by the Board of Aldermen of the Broadway franchise, the Aldermanic office was much sought after. There were many districts in the city, consequently, in which the Republicans, Tammany Hall, and the County Democracy alike assessed Aldermanic candidates from $15 to $25 per election district. Membership in the Assembly is not regarded as so valuable as the Aldermanic office, because the former body is larger, the pay less, the members have to live away from home. It is usual to assess the Assembly candidate from $5 to $15 an election district. The office of State Senator, because it is one of greater influence, and the term is for two years, is much sought for, and the assessments vary from $20 to $30 per election district. In some years the expenditure of Senatorial candidates has been enormous. Thus,

COST OF ELECTIONS IN NEW YORK CITY. 55

when Bradley and O'Brien were running, it is understood that each spent $50,000 in the election. When Morrissey and Schell were running, Morrissey paid an assessment of $10 per election district, while Schell paid one of $50 per election district, and on the night before election paid $2500 to each of the Assembly District leaders in his Senatorial district, to "guarantee the result." We all know how well he succeeded in guaranteeing Morrissey's election. In the last election at which Senators were elected, the Democratic candidates paid $15 for each election district to Tammany Hall, and $15 for each election district to the County Democracy, and $10 for each election district to Irving Hall. Their average assessment was $500 apiece per Assembly District for the County Democracy and Tammany Hall, and $10 per election district for Irving Hall. The Democratic candidates for the Senate alone paid at least $30,000 in assessments.

Candidates for Congress are called upon to pay from $15 to $20 per election district, and when they are nominated by two or all of the organizations, are required to make the same contribution to each organization. When there is no union of the Democratic factions for election of members of Congress, each faction taxes its candidate from $25 to $30 in an election district. Candidates for judicial offices have paid as high as $20,000. From $10,000 to $15,000 is the average assessment for the Superior and Common Pleas bench, while the assessment for the Supreme Court bench has frequently been higher than this. The assessment demanded of the Comptroller at his last election was $10,000. Mayor Hewitt paid $12,000 apiece to the County Democracy and to Tammany Hall, or $24,000. Mr. Edson paid, or there was paid for his account, $10,000 apiece to the County Democracy and Tammany Hall, and $5000 to Irving Hall, or $25,000. Mayor Grace paid $10,000 to the County Democracy when he last ran, and the Citizens' Committee of that year expended about $10,000 of voluntary contributions. In 1880 Mayor Grace paid $12,500 to Irving Hall and $7500 to Tammany Hall. In 1878 Mayor Cooper practically created a party, at what cost to himself he only knows. In 1876 Mayor Ely is reported not to have paid over $5000. John Reilly is said, upon good authority, to have paid Tammany an assessment of $50,000 for the nomination of Register in 1883.

COST OF ELECTIONS IN NEW YORK CITY. 57

An average year would show the following assessments on the basis of two candidates only running in each district, and on the basis of the minimum assessment:

Two Aldermanic candidates at $15 per district for 812 districts....................................	$24,360
Two Assembly candidates at $10 per district for 812 districts.......................................	16,240
Two candidates for Senate or Congress at $25 per election district................................	40,600
Four candidates for Judgeships at $10,000 each.......	40,000
Two candidates for Mayor at $20,000 each............	40,000
Two candidates for a county office such as Sheriff, County Clerk, or Register, at $10,000.....................	20,000
Two candidates for Comptroller at $10,000	20,000
Two candidates for District Attorney at $5000	10,000
Or, say a total of...............................	$211,200

It is a fair estimate, year in and year out, that there is distributed at each polling-place in the 812 districts of the city $75 to $100 by the County Democracy, $75 to $100 by Tammany Hall, $40 to $50 by the Republicans, except in Presidential years, when the distribution has been much larger, $15 by Irving Hall, and $15 by the representatives of the different independent candidates, making a minimum of $220 and a maximum of $280 per election district, which for 812 election districts would give a mean total of $203,000. It is usually calculated that the assessment of candidates will cover this item. At the last election, for example, the County Democracy actually put in the hands of workers at the polls in the Fifteenth Assembly District from $80 to $100 in each election district, and $85 each in the Tenth Assembly District.

As we have seen, the legal election machinery paid ten men for each district at the last election. The minimum, $220 per district, distributed by the party machinery, calculating that $5 was the average paid to each man, although on the total figure this average is too high, and the money is really divided among more people, would provide for 44 men, which, with 10 men paid by law, is 54 men to each of 812 districts, or say 43,848 persons. At the last election 219,992 votes were polled for Mayor, so that over 20 per cent. of all the voters actually received money in one form or another for their election-day services — in a word, were under pay.

In addition to the amount of expenditure at the polls, there is to be calculated the cost of printing, which in different years has ranged in the County Democracy from $12,000 to $19,000 for printing the tickets. To this item there has to be added an expenditure of from $6000 to $8000 for folding, addressing the envelopes, and mailing a set of tickets to each voter in the city. The entire printing bill of each of the three organizations for all purposes whatever is not less than $25,000, or say $75,000 in all, and it certainly costs not less than $25,000 for meetings and miscellaneous expenses for all three parties.

In the campaign of 1882, in which Allan Campbell ran against Franklin Edson, Mr. Campbell's canvass was made in a period of ten days. For the purpose of making that canvas, $63,000 was subscribed, for which Mr. Campbell subscribed $1000, no assessment having been levied; for manning the polls and supplying booths, about $25,000 was expended; for printing the tickets, $10,000; for their distribution by mail, $8000; for advertising, $15,000; for meetings, music, central and local headquarters, and other expenses throughout the city, about $4500. Mr. Butler, the candidate for County Clerk, told me that he personally spent $25,000 in this fight. These figures I give only approximately from memory, but they will serve to show how much money was raised in a canvass in which not one penny, to the knowledge of any member of the Committee, of which I was one, was improperly spent. The Republican party indorsed Mr. Campbell's candidacy, and the Committee was waited upon by a committee from the Republicans, which demanded $15,000 in order to pay the Republican workers at the polls, the same to be distributed among the Republican district leaders. This was objected to. I was subsequently told by two of these leaders that this accounted for Mr. Campbell's defeat. One of them said that he was predisposed to knife Mr. Campbell anyhow, but when he found that we were not willing to contribute, he determined to put the knife in up to the hilt. Another told me that he called his "boys" together, and said they had only $15 per election district in the treasury, that they had made a call on the Independents for more money and had been refused, and asked what had better be done; whereupon they decided unanimously to run Mr. Edson's tickets out of their booths as proper punishment for our niggardliness, although Mr. Campbell was the regular candidate of their party. They might have done as was done by an Assembly District leader of the County Democracy in 1884. He took the money of the County Democracy, and subsequently, for a higher price paid by Tammany Hall, destroyed certain of the tickets for the distribution of which he had been paid by the party.

The expenditures that I have tried to describe in detail have no reference whatever to Presidential or Gubernatorial years. In Presidential years, when we have uniformed parades, fireworks, torch-light processions, great mass-meetings, and a two months' campaign, the amount is increased beyond all believing. In 1884 it cost the County Democracy of the Tenth District $1300 for a single parade in which 1500 men turned out, and only 600 were uniformed. This corresponding item in the Blaine canvass must have been something incredible. The nomination of Cleveland alone cost the County Democracy leaders, who were anxious to play the rôle of Warwicks, over $100,000, as I have been told by some of those leaders with the knowledge that I intended to publish the fact. That sum was made up as follows:

Taking twenty-five men from each Assembly District, with leaders and delegates, to Chicago and back, say six hundred and fifty men, at $22 each	$14,300
Board allowed for six hundred and fifty men, at $10 per day each, for seven days	45,500
So-called parlor expenses, including wine in the committee-room	10,000
Or say	$69,800

the rest having been spent by the six hundred and fifty men for items other than those referred to. Tammany Hall is estimated to have spent about $50,000 on the same pilgrimage.

Neither do the details I have given include expenses in and about bar-rooms, loss of time, and the demoralization of the community. As indicative of how great this latter can be, I would say that I am credibly informed that on the evening of the last great Democratic parade in the late Presidential campaign they took in $2200 for liquors over the Hoffman House bar.

Any one familiar with politics can fix the expenditures in round figures at $100,000 to $125,000 apiece for Tammany Hall and the County Democracy in the average year; $10,000 to $20,000 for Irving Hall; and $50,000 to $75,000 to the Republican party — say a minimum of $265,000, or an average of $307,500; while my calculation of $203,000 distributed in districts, $75,000 for printing and $25,000 for meetings, &c., would give a total of $303,000. In addition to this $307,500 there is to be calculated all of the expenditures of candidates and their friends apart from these contributions to the Machine, a fair estimate of which for the city at large is $100,000; and I believe it to be a minimum estimate, after asking the opinion of a number of district leaders. This will give an item, consequently, of $407,500, to which let us add the $290,000 expended by the city and by the United States, and we will have a grand total in round figures of $700,000 for an average year, and not a Presidential year. The item of $307,500 disbursed by the organizations independent of the personal expenditures of candidates is in excess of the aggregate assessments of candidates, which I estimated at $211,000, and the difference is made good by the assessments on office-holders, levies on public contractors, and contributions from the rich men of the party. The difference of $95,500 to be thus accounted for in all three parties is a most moderate estimate. The Commissionership of Public Works and the Comptrollership are great engines for facilitating this work of subscription and collection, and have been so used to great advantage in the past.

The entire machinery of politics thus pivots on the manner of election, the legal recognition of parties, the ability of parties to levy assessments on office-seekers and office-holders, the practical exclusion, because of the expensiveness of elections, of independent nominations and work, the resulting control of the ballots by Assembly District leaders, and the distribution of ballots to voters on election-day by their subordinates and followers — which, in a word, amounts to a monopoly in the hands of the leaders of the Machines, not only of the power of nomination, but of the elective franchise itself.

CHAPTER IV.
THE EVIL AND THE REMEDY.

THE system of heavy political assessments, and of the employment of large numbers of paid workers at the polls, is of comparatively recent growth. It was between 1860 and 1872 that our municipal politics developed those phases of corruption which have since been a hinderance to the extension of democratic institutions the world over. The characteristic features of the political evils of this period were three: gigantic frauds upon the public treasury, the open use of immense sums of money at the polls, and the almost equally open frauds in polling and canvassing the votes. When the Tweed Ring came into possession of both the political and official machinery of the city, their method was an exceedingly simple one. They distributed the nominations and the offices among themselves, and tapped the public till to pay the expenses of the election. There was no necessity for imposing heavy assessments on candidates, for the organization, as such, did not assume the burden of responsibility for their election in the same way in which it now does. Each candidate looked out for his own election, employed his own men, and he and they spent his or the city's money to carry the day. The sums of money spent were quite as large, if not larger than those spent to-day, but they were not raised by means of assessments, and were not disbursed through the agents of the party machine as such.* Thus, when John McCool ran for Register, in 1864, he paid the highest assessment ever known up to that time, viz., $5000. The successful candidate for Surrogate in 1862 and 1863 paid an assessment of $100 each time, and in 1866, when he was elected for the third time, the fight being exceptionally severe, he was assessed but $2000. It was customary to tax the candidate for the Street Commissionership, in whose office were performed most of the duties now falling upon the Commissioner of Public Works, only $500. When Connolly ran for County Clerk, his assessment was $2500; and when

---

* See Appendix III.

THE EVIL AND THE REMEDY. 67

John Kelly last ran for Sheriff he was assessed only $2000 by the party. He subsequently assessed W. R. Roberts $25,000 for the same office, although it is understood that the latter refused to pay so exorbitant a tax. The aggregate of Tammany's assessments on candidates in 1875, I am told by a member of its Finance Committee of that year, was $162,000, that being the first election after the wages of laborers on the city payrolls had been reduced by Tammany officials to $1.60 per day, and a large fund being needed to make good the defection.

The era of high assessments was ushered in by Mr. Kelly, whose name belongs to history, and whose deeds must be treated by history the same as those of every other man who has filled a large place in public life. He was a great leader and a thorough organizer. No one knew better than he the value of organization, and he centred everything in the organization. He saw the evil of the expenditure of money by candidates, and sought to reduce it by adopting a new system. He induced his party to levy, and its candidates to pay, large assessments, and the organization then assumed the entire responsibility for the result.

This was at the time a decided improvement over the pre-existing state of affairs; ultimately the candidates spent less money and corruption was less rife. This continued to be the case until the factional dissensions in the Democratic party grew to be such as to threaten the permanency of Tammany's power. By this time, as the result of several causes, of which the assessment system was one of the chief, the tendency of the "organization" was to absorb both party feeling and patriotism. The organization came to be everything, and it decided who of its leaders, and in what order, were to be compensated for their service and fealty. Thus it was the custom for years for Tammany to require all who had received office at its hands to practically delegate to it all subordinate appointments. For instance, when vacancies for commissionerships occurred, if Tammany had succeeded in electing its Mayor, the organization would select the man for the vacancy and present his name to the Mayor, who was expected to appoint the nominee. This is the reason why Tammany has fallen out with every Mayor and every Governor since 1872, the last ones always temporarily excepted. Sometimes the organization was sufficiently gracious to submit a small list, and thus afford a narrow margin for selection. In this way each district leader knew that he would be reached in order if he were loyal and energetic. The *esprit de corps* of the machine thus became almost as perfect as that of Napoleon's army. The same tendency was developed in the Republican machine; and when the County Democracy came into existence in 1881, being required to fight a machine so organized, it soon adopted the plan of "fighting the devil with fire." The assessment principle, as well as the principle of the usurpation by the organization of the right to decide which of its members was to be honored by appointment to office, were both adopted to their fullest extent. This was from no motive of fraud or corruption, but because it was the dominant idea of the day, and seemed to be the only plan by which an organization could be created successfully to combat Tammany Hall. The contest between Tammany and the County Democracy resulted naturally enough in both organizations carrying these principles to an extreme. Each needed more money because of the conditions of the conflict, and each increased the assessments. Each required a more marked party loyalty, a more compact organization, and each viewed with greater jealousy all official acts which they required to be done as recognitions of the organization. A Mayor, a Comptroller, a Commissioner of Public Works, or a Police Commissioner could only prove his fidelity to the organization by making his appointments from among those whom the organization and not he had selected. The system thus reached its acme, and it so exists to-day. There is a controversy now pending which perfectly illustrates this state of affairs. By section 1850 of the Consolidation Act, as previously pointed out, the Republican inspectors of elections and poll-clerks are named by the Republican Police Commissioners solely, and the Democratic inspectors and poll-clerks by the Democratic Commissioners. Now, John Simpson is the leader of the Republican district organization of the Sixth Assembly District. Prior to the last election he prepared a list of men whom he desired to be appointed as inspectors and poll-clerks, and presented it to the Republican President of the Board of Police, Mr. S. B. French. There was, however, an opposition to Simpson in his district committee, and the op-

THE EVIL AND THE REMEDY. 71

position also prepared a list which it presented to Commissioner French. The latter divided the appointments between the two factions. This so incensed Simpson's sense of political and legal fairness that he, claiming that as district leader he had an absolute right to name the men to be appointed by the Republican Commissioners, has now preferred charges against the Republican President of the Board of Police to the Republican County Committee, of which both the accuser and accused are members. Mr. French quite naturally and properly answers the charges by saying that the organization has no jurisdiction to try him for his official acts as Police Commissioner. But such a pretension as that of the district leader is the necessary and proper fruit of the political system by which this city is now governed. It has been a gradual growth; but now, having reached its climax, the principles upon which it is founded have become so firmly fixed that even when the organizations merge their differences and act in concert, assessments are levied and workers are employed just as though the Machines were at war, and after the election each organization strives to secure places for itself, and to say who shall fill them, adapting their principles to their claims on the half loaf as they would have done if it were the whole.

All this, however, does not necessarily imply individual corruption on the part of the leaders. It makes corruption easy, but it does not necessitate it. The condition of the law presupposed some machinery or other, not provided for by law, but the Machines have grown stronger than the law. The ultimate result is that one-fifth of our electors are under pay of parties or candidates on election-day; that offices are not unfrequently practically put up at auction to the highest bidder; that public spirit is rendered both hopeless and helpless; and that the members of the Machines alone, and not the people, truly enjoy the benefits of the electoral franchise.

It is not even regarded as an open question in this country whether the State should take any part in so much of the machinery of elections as applies to the manner in which candidates shall be placed in nomination, or the expense of printing and distributing the ballots to the electors shall be borne. Up to the present time all the States of our Union have uniformly decided this question, so far as it has come up for decision, in favor of the non-interference of the State in these particular matters, with the exception of some legislation concerning Primary Elections. Down to about 1870 our own State occupied this same ground, even as to the matter of registration of voters; and even to-day, throughout the rural districts, it is not deemed necessary that the State should interfere to the extent of compelling a registration. It was only the peculiar history of the elections in our own city and in Brooklyn, between the years 1860 and 1870, which compelled the State to depart from this principle of non-interference, to the extent of enacting the general principles of the election laws now in force.

The law thus refuses to take any part in the action of individuals or parties looking to the nomination or election of candidates, other than to see that no person, and he an elector, votes more than once, and that each vote is counted for one and no more. It is apparent, therefore, on its face that if any election is to take place at all in great cities, extra-legal machinery must be brought into existence. Party government is a natural and, I believe, a necessary outgrowth of our constitutional system, and party government can only exist coupled with party machinery, but not necessarily the particular party machinery which we know. The law presumes that the machinery of parties will be sufficient to do, and do in the best possible way, all those things incident to an election, concerning which the law itself is silent. It is unjust and improper, therefore, to condemn our Machines simply because they are Machines. They are blameworthy only in so far *directly* as they are engines of corruption, and *indirectly* as militating against the true spirit of republican institutions. If the law does not compel the public treasury to bear the burden of printing the tickets for an election, which is quite as essential an expenditure as that of supplying the ballot-boxes and the registry of voters, the burden for the payment of which is a public burden, it is because it is assumed that this work will be done voluntarily by individuals. The individuals who do it cannot work singly and alone, but have to work in concert, and the very minute this concert of action is organized you have at least the beginnings of a Machine. It is natural that those who have the greatest stake in the election—that is, the office-holders themselves—should wish to continue in the employment of the Government and to perpetuate their influence. We will assume that every one of them is honestly, earnestly, and patriotically performing the duties of his office, notwithstanding the fact that they act together to make the necessary provision for an essential part of the machinery of elections. The community of their interests welds them into an organized body; the permanency of their interest keeps them practically in the field at all times. They are thus really only devoting themselves to their own business when they are doing what the law expects some citizens, if not all, to do. The merchant, the banker, and the lawyer are no more attending to their business when occupied in their offices than the politician is in attending his club or his committee meetings; and no man can be blamed for attending to his own business, if his business be recognized by law as honest and reputable. One man makes the public business so far his own that the two are treated as practically identical, while the other man's affairs are entirely private in their character and disassociated altogether from those of the public. The great majority of those who, being public servants, are also practically interested in the organization and management of political Machines, are painstaking and careful officers who are actually doing at all times what the law expects all men to do, and what the newspaper press and the general public sentiment is continually asserting all men should do. The Machine really exists as incident to the assumptions of the law which have been spoken of, and it is not necessarily corrupt. The remedy for the evils incident to the existence of the Machines is not by indiscriminately attacking the "practical politicians" and office-holders. This has been done to such an extent that many self-respecting men no longer dare accept office or devote their abilities to the service of the public, either officially or in active politics. That the Machines give birth to corruption and degenerate into engines of evil, there is no room for doubt; but no Machine, as a Machine, is radically blameworthy so long as our law remains as it is. From time to time, Machines organized for temporary purposes spring into existence, conduct campaigns on virtually the same principles as those pursued by the regular Machines, achieve victory or undergo defeat, and then go out of existence. Such Machines are frequently applauded for the good they do, and are rarely condemned, for the reason that they are not permanent, and have not lived long enough to degenerate into corruption or to be a menace to political equality.

We are shocked to think that twenty per cent. of our voters are under pay on election-day; but if the law makes no provision for the payment of men to distribute the ballots, and the Machine finds that it is impossible to get the ballots distributed except by their employment at a fair day's wages, no one can complain. The price paid these men is less, on an average, than that at which the law actually employs its own election officers. Of course, while it is every man's affirmative duty to vote, it is no man's affirmative duty to stand at the polls all day and supply other voters with tickets. In like manner, while it is every man's duty to vote, it is no man's duty to make voluntarily a very heavy expenditure in order to supply the tickets with which other men shall vote. The party organizations, acting as such, whether from patriotic or other motives, volunteer to do the duty which the law assumes will be done somehow or other. The funds for the payment of the expense absolutely and necessarily incident to legal election must be found in some way, and they are naturally found by the men most interested in the result—party leaders, office-holders, and candidates for office. It is natural, therefore, that they should, as "practical" men, come to regard themselves and not the public as the true beneficiaries of our political system.

Although it is certain that in this city much of the money raised by organizations has from time to time been misappropriated by the men who have collected and have been relied upon to disburse it, it is nevertheless true that far the greater part of this money has been disposed of for the purposes for which it was raised, and which the law does not condemn.

The real and justifiable objections to the Machines are that they exist in perpetuity, and that their leaders come to possess a monopoly of the means for supplying the necessary extra-legal machinery of the election. Possessing these means, they have to be sought by any one desiring a nomination; and as a condition precedent to acting in any one's behalf, they can insist upon contributions to their exchequer such as they see fit to impose. These are the *positive* evils of the Machine, which tend naturally to corruption, because they put a premium on it. The *negative* evils are, that to conduct an election in opposition to the Machines a machinery of much the same kind has to be adopted, involving almost equally large expense, and calling upon its leaders and subordinates for an amount of attention and care, loss of time and contributions of money, that ultimately amount to an absolute deterrent from political activity, except upon rare and unusual occasions. The Machines are thus left in practical sole occupancy of the field, and so far hold a monopoly of the elective franchise that in this city any two of the three can, by uniting, make the election of their candidates a foregone conclusion. So true is this that they can, by combination, guarantee the election of candidates chosen at hazard from a hat, or defeat almost any law that can be conceived providing for the representation of minorities.

In 1873, when the present charter of this city was enacted, the design was to provide for minority representation in electing the Board of Aldermen, where it was believed to be peculiarly needed. The law, however, was completely nullified by the possibility of co-operation among parties. Thus it was only necessary at any time for any two of the three Machines to agree as to which candidates they would vote for, dividing them among themselves, and having their tickets printed accordingly, to make the election absolutely certain. Consequently, instead of providing minority representation, the law afforded the opportunity for guaranteeing the result of combinations between parties, thus making them, because of the assurance of success, almost completely irresponsible for their nominations. This is only one of the many ways in which it is possible for the election machinery existing in virtue of the theory of the law that elections will be voluntarily conducted, to defeat the whole purpose of popular elections.

The remedies for the tyranny and irresponsibility of the Machines have been under discussion ever since the evils first became evident. It is asserted continually that the only remedy is an enlivened and enlightened public spirit. For many years the pulpit and the press have been calling upon the people to awake to a realization of their political duties. Once in a great while public spirit is sufficiently aroused to accomplish something of good, and then dies out again. From time to time new organizations spring into existence with the view of becoming permanent. At first, as new Machines free from corruption, they declare war against the older and corrupter ones and do good work; but if they live long enough, they invariably fall into the habits and methods of all Machines whatsoever, because those habits and methods are absolutely incident to the life of political organizations under existing conditions. Some would have us believe that sporadic movements and temporary Machines, having so frequently proved a failure, are not to be relied on, but that the Machine should be supplemented by a sort of organization within the organization, which shall watch the manner in which the party subordinates perform their duties. This may be illustrated by the suggestion which I have frequently heard, that while it is necessary for both the Republican and Democratic parties to fully man the polls on election-day with paid workers, there should be another set of volunteer patriots who should devote themselves to seeing that the paid workers do their duty and faithfully earn their pay. But this raises the old, old question, *Quis custodiet ipsos custodes ?*

For the purpose of meeting the corruption which has prevailed in the matter of nominations and preventing frauds at Primary Elections, the law has departed from its principle of non-interference, and has recognized and sanctioned the extra-legal machinery incident to placing candidates in nomination by primary meetings. This is a radical departure from the general theory of the law, and has so far almost wholly failed in securing any real improvement in the condition of affairs, because the most honestly conducted primary is, after all, only a primary of the enrolled or recognized members of a party availing themselves of the machinery supplied by the party. In the long-run the majority at a primary meeting represents the party, and under the existing systems of organization the party is for the purposes of the Machine, as the Machine is for the purposes of the party, nothing more than a number of autocratic leaders. Reform by the legal recognition of the Machines is, consequently, not only a failure, but directly perpetuates the evil by the sanction implied in its recognition.

THE EVIL AND THE REMEDY. 83

The last noteworthy fight by an independent organization that has recently been made in this city against the dominant Machines was in 1882, when the Independent party had the nominal aid and backing of the Republican organization, and it nevertheless cost $63,000 to conduct the election. So long as the law remains unchanged, I do not believe that it would be possible to have an independent municipal canvass in this city at an expenditure of less than that amount, unless the movement were to be conducted in concert with some already thoroughly organized and well-distributed body of citizens, such, for instance, as the labor organizations which used their machinery in the late canvass, in which Mr. George polled so phenomenal a vote. Even then the expense is very large—so large as for a long time to have been a very serious deterrent to the attempt on the part of the labor organizations to act in concert in any municipal movement.

Besides vesting the power of nomination in fee-simple in those persons who practically own the machinery for printing and distributing the ballots, the existing system amounts to an almost complete exclusion from official public life of all men who are not enabled to pay, if not a sum equal to the entire salary of the office they seek, at least a very large percentage of it. The poor man or the moderately well-to-do man is thus at once cut off from all political ambition, because the only key to success is wealth or machine power. The ablest lawyer at our bar could not secure a nomination for a judgeship unless he were able to pay an assessment of from $10,000 to $20,000, while a mere political lawyer, if he have the means of paying his assessment and stands well with the party leaders, can without great difficulty secure a nomination and even an election to an office for which he has no peculiar qualifications.

When, under the old system, the evil became unbearable, our present election and registration laws were enacted. There is to-day another evil equally unbearable, due, as the old evil was due, to the insufficiency of the election laws, and those laws will again have to be changed, not by undoing anything that has been done, but by extending their application, and by having the State or city take into its own hands all the machinery of elections whatever. All other suggested remedies will prove futile, or at best only temporary. The result of this will be that Machines will no longer have to be fought by Machines, or by an aroused public spirit, or by appointing watchers to watch the watchers. Public spirit will have so fair a chance that it will be awake at all times. If a method can be found by which all men and all Machines can be given political equality before the law, actually as well as theoretically, the evil will die a natural death. If the city were to print and distribute the ballots, the result would be that the organizations, no longer having control of the machinery required for these purposes, would, as a consequence, no longer have control of the power of nomination and levying assessments. The mainspring of the Machine would be shattered. Enlightened public spirit would be no less necessary than now. It would be strengthened and confirmed by the opportunity offered it by the law to really and at all times count for something. A poor man would have as good an opportunity as a rich man, and the independent as fair a chance as the partisan.

While, as a rule, social evils are more difficult of treatment than any others, because of the complexity of the facts and the difficulty in locating their causes, it is true that if the causes be once clearly defined, the evil is already in a fair way to cure itself. It suggests its own remedy. Let us therefore try to summarize distinctly the causes of the evil, and note the remedies which they naturally suggest.

THE EVIL.	THE REMEDY.
1. The necessity for voluntarily printing and distributing the ballot justifies organization for this purpose.	1. The *printing* and *distribution* of all ballots at public expense does away with the necessity of organization for this purpose.
2. It practically vests the Machines with the monopoly of the election machinery.	2. And will deprive the political Machines of the monopoly of an essential part of the election machinery.
3. And, as a consequence, with the monopoly of nomination.	3. It will enable any body of citizens of the number prescribed by law to have the name of their candidate printed on the same ballot with the names of all other candidates for the same office, so that before the law and before the voters all candidates and all party organizations will stand on a perfectly even footing.
4. It involves the necessity of defraying the expenses of both printing and distribution by means of assessments on or contributions by candidates, officeholders, or party leaders.	4. This will dispense altogether with the necessity of and excuse for levying political assessments.

THE EVIL AND THE REMEDY.

THE EVIL.	THE REMEDY.
5. Which facilitates bribery and corruption by affording them convenient covers.	5. And leave no legal cover for bribery. The law can describe and limit all permissible expenditure, and compel the candidate or his agent to make a sworn return with vouchers to a proper public officer for all disbursements. It may punish all violations with sufficiently severe penalties.
6. And debauches the electors by leading them to become partisans for pay instead of honestly and from conviction performing their duty as citizens.	6. And prescribe that no elector under pay of a party or candidate shall be permitted to vote, thus making it more the interest of candidates and parties not to pay than to pay for election services, and thus deterring all honest electors from accepting pay.

These are the remedies naturally suggested by the evil, whereas all other suggested remedies are either the nostrums of political quacks, the dreams of inexperienced enthusiasts, or measures of partial relief attacking the symptoms only and not the causes of the evil. Almost all of the remedies which are suggested from time to time are wholly experimental, the results of which for good or ill can only be guessed and not known. If the same could be said of the remedies, the necessity for which is disclosed by an intimate and thorough knowledge of the wrongs to be cured, we should all feel towards them as we do towards the others, that is, we should doubt and mistrust them to the point of letting them go untried, rather than run the risk of intensifying or changing the character of the evils of which we complain. As matter of fact, however, these suggested remedies are not untried or experimental. They have been tried, and have already accomplished exactly the result to be expected of them.

A careful study of the English law of elections, the Ballot Acts and the Prevention of Corrupt Practices Acts, will not only suggest how our own law can be modified, but will in many respects, *mutatis mutandis*, afford a good guide in drafting the legislation needed to embody and apply the remedy. In addition to this it will show how completely impossible it is, under such a law as that which prevails in Great Britain, for the evils from which we suffer to be perpetuated a single day. After we have studied these laws in operation elsewhere, and considered the changes necessary to conform them to our own system, we shall be prepared not only to solve the great and difficult problem of excluding fraud and corruption from municipal politics, but how to supply a means of actually divorcing municipal from state and national politics, and of opening the way to the best attainable administration of our municipal business, which, while it bears no natural relation to party politics, is to-day almost entirely sacrificed to it, and made a mere counter in the game of personal or political ambition.

CHAPTER V.

THE REMEDY AS APPLIED IN ENGLAND.

THE whole of our existing political machinery in the city of New York being shown to be incident to the fact that the laws anticipate some extra-legal means for printing and distributing the ballots, only one question remains to be asked, viz., What are the practical suggestions as to the manner in which the law should provide for the performance of these functions?

The English Ballot Act of 1872 affords a most practical and admirable model. This act provides that at every poll at an election the vote shall be given by ballot; that the ballot of each voter shall contain the names and description of all the candidates for the particular office for which he is voting, which ballot paper has a number printed on the back of it, and is attached to a stub, or "counter-foil," as it is called, with the same number printed on the face of the stub. At the time

THE REMEDY AS APPLIED IN ENGLAND 91

of voting, the ballot paper is marked on both sides with an official mark, and delivered to the voter at the polling-place. All voters are registered before each election, and when the voter has registered he is given a registration number. This registration number is marked on the stub of the ballot at the time the ballot is delivered to him; the voter then marks his vote on the ballot, which he so folds as to conceal his mark, and casts it in the box in the presence of the officer or inspector of elections, after having shown him the official mark on the back of the ballot, this being done for the purpose of enabling the inspector to identify the ballot as a legal ballot, distributed by the proper officer. If any ballot is cast without the official mark, or if, in the canvass, it appears that any voter has voted for more candidates than he has a right to, or if the ballot is so written upon or marked that the voter himself can be identified by reference to the ticket, it is to be treated as void, and not counted by the canvassers.

Our own law with regard to the counting and canvassing of the vote cannot be improved. Were we to avail of the English experience, we should have to establish alongside of or in our polling-place on election-day another place to which each voter could go and get his ticket. This function of distributing the tickets would be performed by two or more officers, appointed in the same general manner in which the other officers of election, say poll-clerks and inspectors, are appointed. The tickets would be printed by the Bureau of Elections, however constituted, in the same manner in which all the other blanks and papers incident to election are now printed.

Under the English law it is only necessary for any ten persons who desire to vote for a candidate for a municipal office to make a certificate to that effect. When such certificate is filed with the proper officer, it becomes his duty to print the name of such candidate upon the common ballot. It would probably be necessary, because of the denseness of the population in this city and the immense vote cast, to limit the right of nomination by certificate in this way to at least fifty electors for district officers, and a greater number for officers running in the city at large. All such nominations should be required to be made within at least fifteen days before the election, after which time no further nominations could be made. The

THE REMEDY AS APPLIED IN ENGLAND. 93

Bureau of Elections should be required to publish in the *City Record* all nominations thus certified at least two days before the third registration-day, inasmuch as the number of electors who register and vote is always largely governed by the character of the nominees. The election officers would then proceed to get up the tickets and stubs as required by law, leaving a blank place on each ticket to be used by the voter in case he wish to vote for any one other than the certified candidates.

The following would be the form of the face of the ballot paper and of the stub from which it is torn when delivered to the voter:

Stub.		Ballot.
Stub No.... (NOTE.—The stub is to have a number to correspond with that on the back of the ballot.)	1	BROWN. John Brown of ——— East Tenth Street. Tailor.
	2	JOHNS. Peter Johns of ——— Broadway. Merchant.
	3	CLARK. Thaddeus Clark of ——— West Twelfth Street. Printer.
	4	Sherman. George Henry Sherman of ——— ——— ——— Street. Lawyer.
	5	

Thus, if we were to adopt this system for any aldermanic election in the Twentieth Assembly District, for instance, any fifty electors could place whomsoever they please in nomination, and his name would be printed with the names of all other persons so nominated upon a common ticket. This ticket being printed and distributed at public expense, and the names of all candidates alike coming before every voter with perfect impartiality and absolute fairness, the Machine would lose its entire value, because the nomination of any fifty citizens would be just as good, just as valuable, as the nominations of the strongest organizations. The room for organized work would be only such as was left for a fair and proper canvass of the district prior to the election, and on election-day for the purpose of securing the most votes possible for each candidate.

The following is the form of directions for the guidance of the voter in voting, which is required by the English law to be printed in conspicuous characters and placarded in every polling-station and in every compartment of every polling-station:

"The voter may vote for —— candidates. The voter will go into one of the compartments (which

THE REMEDY AS APPLIED IN ENGLAND.

are like simple booths temporarily set up at each distribution-place), and with a pencil provided in the compartment, place a cross on the right-hand side opposite the name of each candidate for whom he votes, thus: +. The voter will then fold up the ballot paper, so as to show the official mark on the back, and leaving the compartment, will, without showing the front of the paper to any person, show the official mark on the back to the presiding officer (the inspector), and then in the presence of the presiding officer put the paper into the ballot-box and forthwith quit the polling-station. If the voter inadvertently spoils a ballot paper, he can return it to the officer, who will, if satisfied of such inadvertence, give him another paper.

"If the voter votes for more than —— candidate, or places any mark on the paper by which he may be afterwards identified, his ballot paper will be void and will not be counted.

"If the voter takes a ballot paper out of the polling-station, or deposits in the ballot-box any other paper than the one given him by the officer, he will be guilty of a misdemeanor, and be subject to imprisonment for any term with or without hard labor."

The schedule adds the following: "*Note.*—These directions shall be illustrated by examples of the ballot paper."

Of course, the form of directions here would be made to conform to the particular provisions of our own statute as to penalties, etc., as they might be prescribed.

The English rules for the conduct of the election require that proper polling-places shall be provided by the proper officers in much the same way that our own law provides for the leasing of proper places by the Bureau of Elections. The election officers are required to provide the polling-place with materials to mark the ballot papers, with instruments for stamping the official mark upon them, and with copies of a registry of voters or of such part thereof as contains the names of the voters allotted to vote at such station. They are required to keep the official mark secret.

In our own system not only is the register of voters always present on election-day, but if extra registers are needed for any purpose whatever, they are easily had, in view of the fact that before election the entire registry is printed by Assembly Districts in the *City Record*. Under the Eng-

THE REMEDY AS APPLIED IN ENGLAND. 97

lish system, the officer designated by law is required, on the application of any voter who is incapacitated by blindness or any other physical cause from voting in the manner prescribed by law, or of any voter who makes declaration that he is unable to read, to cause the vote of such voter to be marked on the ballot paper in such manner as the voter directs, in the presence of the agents of the several candidates, if they desire to be present, and the ballot paper to be placed in the ballot-box. The name and number of every voter whose vote is marked in pursuance of this rule, and the reason why it is so marked, is required to be entered on a list known to the law as "the list of votes marked by the election officer." The declaration of inability to read is required to be made by the voter, at the time of voting, before the presiding officer at the election, who is required to attest it. Any voter who has inadvertently dealt with his ballot in such a manner as that it cannot be conveniently used as a ballot paper, may, upon delivering it to the ballot officer, obtain another ballot paper in the place of the one so delivered up, and the spoiled ballot paper is required to be immediately cancelled.

7

It is needless to go into minor details. It is quite sufficient to point out these general features. Our existing law would not require great modification or many amendments to incorporate into it the best and most material features of this system. If it were done, the plea for assessments, because of the necessity of providing an extra-legal machinery for printing and distributing the ballot, would at once disappear; the immense tax, which is now unequally borne by the electors, would be borne by all alike, because these expenditures are as entirely public in their character as the expenditures for registration or canvassing the ballots.

It would only be necessary to go one step further to remove the last great opportunity or opening for fraud or corruption in the contribution or use of money. The foregoing suggestions, if adopted and added to our existing laws, would make them include, as they should, the entire machinery of elections. But even if all of this machinery were under the control of the State it would still be possible for organizations and candidates, by the lavish and corrupt use of money, to secure the election by the purchase of votes. No country in the world has probably ever suf-

THE REMEDY AS APPLIED IN ENGLAND.

fered more from this evil than England, and we may well profit by its experience.

There the first act for the prevention of corrupt practices was passed in 1854. It has been followed by a number of others of an amendatory character. All elections are now conducted under the general provisions of the Corrupt and Illegal Practices Act of 1883.

The Municipal Corporations Act of 1882, by section 75, provides that a person guilty of corrupt practices at a municipal election shall be liable to the like actions, prosecutions, penalties, forfeitures, and punishments, as if the corrupt practice had been committed at a Parliamentary election. The provisions of the Corrupt Practice Preventions acts of 1854, 1858, and 1863 and 1883, are thus made directly applicable to municipal and borough elections.

The first of these acts as amended starts out with a definition of BRIBERY which is so much fuller and better than that of our own law as to justify its quotation. The following persons are declared to be guilty of bribery:

"1. Every person who shall directly or indirectly by himself or by any other person on his behalf give, lend, or agree to give or lend, or shall offer, promise, or promise to procure, or to endeavor to procure any money or valuable consideration to or for any voter, or to or for any person on behalf of any voter, or to or for any other person in order to induce any voter to vote or refrain from voting, or shall corruptly do any such act as aforesaid on account of such voter having voted or refrained from voting at an election.

"2. Every person who shall directly or indirectly by himself or by any other person on his behalf give or procure, or agree to give or procure, or offer or promise to procure, or to endeavor to procure any office, place, or employment, to or for any voter, or to or for any person on behalf of any voter, or to or for any other person, in order to induce such voter to vote or refrain from voting, or shall corruptly do any act as aforesaid on account of any voter having voted or refrained from voting at any election.

"3. Every person who shall directly or indirectly by himself or by any other person on his behalf make any such gift, loan, offer, promise, procurement, or agreement as aforesaid to or for any person in order to induce such person to procure or

THE REMEDY AS APPLIED IN ENGLAND. 101

endeavor to procure the return of any person to serve in Parliament (or any municipal office) or the vote of any voter at any election.

"4. Every person who shall upon or in consequence of any such gift, loan, offer, promise, procurement, or agreement, procure or engage, promise or endeavor to procure the return of any person to serve in Parliament (or any municipal office) or the vote of any voter at any election.

"5. Every person who shall advance or pay, or cause to be paid any money to or to the use of any other person, with the intent that such money or any part thereof shall be expended in bribery at any election, or who shall knowingly pay or cause to be paid any money to any person in discharge or repayment of any money wholly or in part expended in bribery at any election.

"Provided always that the aforesaid enactment shall not extend or be construed to extend to any money paid or agreed to be paid for or on account of any legal expenses *bona fide* incurred at or concerning any election. The following persons are deemed guilty of bribery :

"1. Every voter who shall before or during any election, directly or indirectly, by himself or by any other person on his behalf receive, agree, or contract for any money, gift, loan, or valuable consideration, office, place or employment for himself or for any other person, for voting or agreeing to vote, or for refraining or agreeing to refrain from voting at any election.

"2. Every person who shall at any election, directly or indirectly, by himself or by any other person on his behalf, receive any money or valuable consideration on account of any person for voting or refraining from voting or having induced any other person to vote or refrain from voting at any election."

TREATING is defined by the Act of 1883:

"1. Any person who corruptly by himself or by any other person either before, during, or after an election directly or indirectly gives, or provides, or pays wholly or in part the expense of giving or providing any meat, drink, entertainment, or provision to or for any person for the purpose of corruptly influencing that person or any other person to give or refrain from giving his vote at the election or on account of such person or any other person having voted, or refrained from voting, or being about to vote or refrain from voting at such election, shall be guilty of treating.

"2. And every elector who corruptly accepts or takes any such meat, drink, entertainment, or provision shall also be guilty of treating."

UNDUE INFLUENCE is defined as follows:

"Every person who shall directly or indirectly by himself or by any other person on his behalf make use of or threaten to make use of any force, violence, or restraint, or inflict or threaten to inflict by himself or by any other person, any temporal or spiritual injury, damage, harm, or loss upon or against any person, in order to induce or compel such person to vote or refrain from voting, or on account of such person having voted or refrained from voting at any election, or who shall by abduction, duress, or any fraudulent device or contrivance impede or prevent the free exercise of the franchise of any elector, or shall thereby compel, induce, or prevail upon any elector either to give or to refrain from giving his vote at any election, shall be guilty of undue influence."

It will be noticed that every possible form of corruption at an election, commonly referred to in this country as bribery, is covered by these definitions of bribery and treating. As to the provision against undue influence, if we were to adopt it, it would put an end to numberless evils which now tend to defeat a free election, such as the compulsion of employés by their employers to vote for any particular person, no matter how cunningly such compulsion were to be disguised, the threat of discipline by a party Machine, club, or other political or social organization, or the threat to boycott or expel from a trade-union or other labor organization any person refusing to vote as such organization might dictate, or any religious influence whatever. The necessity for some such legislation is urgent, although it must be admitted to be difficult of procurement at the hands of our Legislatures.

The law provides proper penalties for each of the foregoing offences, as well as for the false and fraudulent personation, or the procurement of the personation, of any elector. These may be described as the great or major corrupt practices. The minor corrupt practices are referred to in the succeeding sections of the statute, thus:

Sec. 7 of the Act prescribes—

"1. No payment or contract for payment shall

THE REMEDY AS APPLIED IN ENGLAND. 105

for the purpose of promoting or procuring the election of a candidate at any election, be made—

"(*a*) On account of the conveyance of electors to or from the poll, whether for the hiring of horses or carriages, or for railway fares or otherwise (but electors are permitted to hire conveyance for themselves in common), or

"(*b*) To an elector on account of the use of any house, land, building, or premises for the exhibition of any address, bill, or notice, or on account of the exhibition of any address, bill, or notice.

"(*c*) On account of any committee-room in excess of the number allowed by the first schedule to this Act.

"2. Subject to such exception as may be allowed in pursuance of this Act. If any payment or contract for payment is knowingly made in contravention of this section either before, during, or after an election, the person making such payment or contract shall be guilty of an illegal practice, and any person receiving such payment or being a party to any such contract, knowing the same to be in contravention of this Act, shall also be guilty of an illegal practice.

"3. Provided that where it is the ordinary business of an elector, as an advertising agent, to accept for payment bills and advertisements, a payment to or contract with such elector, if made in the ordinary course of business, shall not be deemed to be an illegal practice."

Section 8 prescribes generally that subject to such exception as is allowed in pursuance of the act no sum shall be paid and no expense shall be incurred by a candidate at an election, or by his election agent, whether before, during, or after the election, on account of or in respect to the conduct or management of such election, in excess of the maximum amount specified in the first schedule of the act; and any candidate or any election agent who knowingly acts in contravention of these provisions is held to be guilty of an illegal practice.

When a person knowingly provides money for any entertainment contrary to the provisions of the act, or for any expenses incurred in excess of the maximum amount allowed by the act, or for replacing any money expended in such payment or expenses except as allowed in pursuance of the act, he is guilty of an illegal payment. A person convicted of an illegal practice under the foregoing sections of the act is liable to a fine not exceeding $500, and is incapable of being registered as an elector for the period of five years.

Any person who corruptly induces or procures a candidate to withdraw from being a candidate at any election in consideration of the payment or promise of payment, as well as any person withdrawing in pursuance of such an agreement, is guilty of the offence of illegal payment.

No payment or contract for payment for the purpose of promoting or procuring the election of a candidate at any election is permitted to be made on account of bands of music, torches, flags, banners, cockades or ribbons, or other marks of distinction. Any person making any payment for such purpose is guilty of an illegal payment, and any person being a party to such contract or receiving such payment is also held to be guilty of illegal payment, if he knew the same to be contrary to law.

No person is permitted, for the purpose of promoting or procuring the election of a candidate, to be engaged or employed for payment or promise of payment for any purpose or in any capacity whatever, except for the purpose or capacity mentioned in the schedules of the act. Any person so employed, or any person so employing another, is guilty of illegal employment.

Every bill, placard, or poster having reference to the election is required to have the name and address of the printer and publisher thereof on its face.

No premises on which the sale by wholesale or retail of intoxicating liquors is authorized by license, or where intoxicating liquor is sold or supplied to members of a club, society, or association other than a permanent political club, or wherein refreshments of any kind, whether meat or drink, are ordinarily supplied for sale on the premises, or any public elementary school building, is permitted to be used as a committee-room for the purpose of promoting or procuring the election of a candidate at an election; and if any person hires or uses any such premises or any part thereof for a committee-room, he is guilty of illegal hiring as well as the person letting such premises, if he knew the purposes for which they were intended to be used. The section, however, does not apply to any part of premises ordinarily used for chambers or the holding of public meetings, provided

THE REMEDY AS APPLIED IN ENGLAND.

such part of the premises has a separate entrance, and has no direct communication with any part of the premises in which liquors or refreshments are sold.

On or before the day of nomination a person is required to be named by or on behalf of each candidate as his agent for such election, and the candidate may name himself as his own election agent, and thereupon become subject to the provisions of the law, both as candidate and as election agent. The name and address of the election agent of each candidate is required, on or before the day of nomination, to be notified in writing by the candidate, or some one in his behalf, to the returning officer (or say the Bureau of Elections), who is required to give public notice of the name and address of every agent so declared. This could here be published in the *City Record* at a minimum of expense. No candidate is permitted to appoint more than one election agent, but the candidate may revoke the appointment of his agent, in which event he is required to certify such revocation and the new appointment to the returning officer.

An election agent of a candidate is permitted to

appoint a number of deputies or sub-agents to act in different election districts. One full day before the election the election agent is required to declare in writing the name and address of every sub-agent to the returning officer (or inspector), who shall make the same public. The election agents of a candidate are required, either by themselves or their sub-agents, to appoint all polling agents (or what correspond to our workers at the polls), clerks, and messengers employed for payment in behalf of the candidate at an election, and hired through or on behalf of a candidate.

Except as permitted by the act, no payment and no advance or deposit is permitted to be made by the candidate, or by any agent on behalf of the candidate, or any other person, at any time, whether before, during, or after the election, in respect to any expense incurred on account of or in respect to the conduct or management of such election, otherwise than by or through the election agent of the candidate, whether acting in person or by sub-agents.

Every payment in excess of forty shillings is required to be vouched for by a receipted bill stating the particulars. All expenses at an election

THE REMEDY AS APPLIED IN ENGLAND. 111

are required to be paid within the time limited by the act, which is twenty-eight days after the day on which the candidates returned are declared elected.

The candidate at any parliamentary election is permitted to pay any personal expenses incurred by him on account of or in connection with or incidental to such election to an amount not exceeding one hundred pounds, but any further personal expenses are required to be paid by his election agent. The candidate is required to send to his election agent within the time limited by the act a statement of the amount of his personal expenses paid by himself.

Any person may, if authorized in writing by the election agent, pay necessary expenses for stationery, postage, etc., to a total amount not exceeding that named in the authority.

Within thirty-five days after the day on which the candidates returned at the election are declared elected, the election agent of every candidate is required to transmit to the returning officer a true return in the form prescribed by the second schedule of the act.

(*a*) A statement of all payments made by the

election agent, together with all the bills and receipts.

(*b*) A statement of the amount of personal expenses, if any, paid by the candidate.

(*c*) A statement of the sums paid to the returning officer for his charges. (We here would have no such item.)

(*d*) A statement of all disputed claims of which the election agent is aware.

(*e*) A statement of all the unpaid claims, if any, of which the election agent is aware.

(*f*) A statement of all moneys, securities, and equivalent of money received by the election agent from the candidate or any other person for the purpose of expenses incurred, or to be incurred, or in respect of the conduct or management of the election, with a statement of the name of every person from whom the same have been received.

This return is required to be accompanied by a declaration made under oath by the election agent before a justice of the peace. Where the candidate has named himself as his own election agent, he is required to make a like return. At the time the agent transmits the return, or within seven days afterwards, the candidate is required to transmit

THE REMEDY AS APPLIED IN ENGLAND. 113

to the returning officer a sworn declaration setting out the fact of his nomination, and declaring that he has taken no part whatever in the election, and further solemnly and sincerely declaring that he has not, and no person, club, society, or association at his expense has, made any payment or given or promised or offered any reward, office, employment, or valuable consideration, or incurred any liability on account of or in respect to the conduct or management of the election, and further that he has not paid any money or given any security or equivalent for money to the person acting as his agent, or to any person, club, society, or association, on account of the conduct or management of the election, and that he is entirely ignorant of any money, security, or equivalent for money having been paid, advanced, given, or deposited by any one for the purpose of defraying any expenses incurred on account of his election; and he further solemnly and sincerely declares that he will not at any future time, except so far as permitted by law, make or be a party to the making or giving of any payment, reward, office, employment, or valuable consideration for the purpose of defraying any expenses at the election, or to provide or be a party to the providing of any money, security, or equivalent for money for the purpose of defraying such expenses.

A declaration of the same general character is required to be made by the election agent, declaring that no moneys have been spent other than those contained in his return of election expenses.

The returning officer at every election, within ten days after he receives from the election agent the return of expenses, is required to publish a summary of the returns of expenses in not less than two newspapers circulating in the county or borough for which the election was held, accompanied by a notice of the time and place at which the returns and declarations can be inspected, and they charge the candidate with the expense of such publication.

The returning officer (here it would have to be the Bureau of Elections) keeps the return of the expenses and declarations at his office, or at some convenient place which he designates, for two years following the election.

All persons guilty of corrupt or illegal practice are disqualified from voting.

General provision is made for the hearing of

THE REMEDY AS APPLIED IN ENGLAND. 115

persons before they are found guilty of corrupt or illegal practice. All registration officers are required to keep a list of all persons incapacitated from voting because of having been found guilty of corrupt or illegal practice under the statute.

The act provides for regular proceedings and the trial in the Central Criminal Court on indictments for corrupt practice at the instance of the Attorney-general; contains special provisions requiring witnesses to answer truly all questions which they are required to answer by the Election Court, *and no witness is excused from answering any question relating to any offence at or connected with an election* on the ground that the answer would tend to incriminate them, but no such answer can in any proceeding, civil or criminal, be admitted in evidence against the witness, except in case of a criminal proceeding for perjury in respect to such evidence.

The candidate is declared to be any person who is nominated as a candidate at such election, or is declared by himself or by others to be a candidate after the issue of the writ for the election; but if he is nominated by others without his consent, nothing in the act shall be so construed as to impose upon him any liability as a candidate unless he afterwards gives his assent to the nomination.

Part I. of the first schedule refers to the persons who may be legally employed for payment:

1. One election agent, and no more.

2. One deputy election agent for each polling district, and no more.

3. One polling agent for each polling station, and no more. In a borough (which corresponds to one of our cities) one clerk and one messenger for every 500 electors in the borough.

In applying the principles of the act to this city these figures, of course, would have to be much modified.

The act further prescribes that any paid election agent, sub-agent, polling agent, clerk, or messenger may or may not be an elector, but he may not vote.

Part II. refers to election expenses in addition to the expenses in Part I., and limits them to—

1. Certain sums paid to the returning officer in conformity with the law.

2. Personal expenses of the candidate.

THE REMEDY AS APPLIED IN ENGLAND. 117

3. Expenses of printing, advertising, publishing, issuing, and distributing addresses and notices.

4. Expenses of stationery, messengers, postage, and telegrams.

5. Expense of holding public meetings.

6. In a borough the expense of committee-room, not to exceed one committee-room for each 500 electors.

7. In the county the expenses of a central committee-room.

Part III. provides that the expenses for miscellaneous matters other than those mentioned in Parts I. and II. shall not, on the whole, amount to a maximum of more than £200.

Part IV. provides a maximum scale of permissible expenditures. In a borough the expenses mentioned in Parts I., II., and III. of the schedule other than personal expenses and sums paid to the returning officer for charges under the law, shall not exceed on the whole a maximum amount, as follows:

If the number of electors on the registry does not exceed 2000, the maximum amount shall be £350.

If it does exceed 2000, £380, and an additional

£30 for every complete 1000 electors in addition to the 2000.

If it is found that a corrupt practice has been committed with the knowledge and consent of the candidate, he is forever disqualified from holding office, and is deprived of his franchise as an elector. If such corrupt practice is found to have occurred by the act of the agent with or without the candidate's knowledge and consent, the candidate himself is disqualified from serving during the time for which he was elected, and can neither hold office nor act as an elector for seven years. Similar penalties are imposed on agents and subagents found guilty. These penalties are all in addition to penalties of fines and imprisonment after conviction on an indictment of bribery, undue influence, treating, illegal payments, or other corrupt practices.

This system has finally so eliminated the opportunities and the possibilities of fraud and corruption in the use of money as practically to have put an end to them, if it be considered what they have been any time the last hundred years.*

---

* See Appendix IV.

The application of some such a system to our own elections in combination with a system providing for the printing and distribution of tickets at the public expense (and our present election laws could be readily amended in such a manner as to avail of all of the best suggestions of the English system without complicating the elections, and without running counter to any honest public sentiment) would remove every one of the foundation stones that lie at the base of our present organized political machinery. It might be impracticable to adopt these laws as applicable to municipal elections alone, without changing the time of the election, in view of the fact that municipal elections now take place simultaneously with state or national elections. Either the law would have to be adopted for all elections whatever throughout the State, or else the municipal elections would have to take place at some time other than that provided for state and national elections. The opinion has long prevailed among the most thoughtful men in our great cities that the charter election should take place in the spring. The answer to this, so far as any answer has been possible, has invariably been that the charter election, as a rule, does not elicit sufficient public interest to call out the entire vote of the city; that such being the case the only vote which would come out would be the organized Machine vote, and that in that event we should be even worse off than we now are. It is contended that the advantage of having the general and charter elections take place simultaneously is that the largest possible number of voters come to the polls, and being there, vote on municipal as well as general issues. This objection to spring elections has been sought to be answered by saying that some provision for minority representation would entirely overcome it. At the last session of the Legislature a bill for spring elections in the city of New York was passed, and provision was made for minority representation. Although the Governor believed in the principle of a spring election, he, nevertheless, found himself compelled to veto the bill because of the provisions providing for minority representation, and this was justified in view of the fact that minority representation is a mere delusion and snare so long as parties are organized and permitted to exist as at present. If the objection to spring elections be that the great body of voters would not vote, and

THE REMEDY AS APPLIED IN ENGLAND.

that the Machines would be more powerful under such circumstances than they even now are, provisions for minority representation under our present election laws would only intensify the evil; because, even if the entire voting population came out, the party Machines could foreclose the possibility of defeat by combination, and thus be practically irresponsible as to the candidates whom they should nominate.

All of these difficulties would, however, be overcome if in the municipal election the Machine were paralyzed through the deprivation by law of its present monopoly of printing and distributing the tickets, and if an act similar to the English Act for the prevention of corrupt practices were to be enacted, thus disfranchising all persons who took money in working as canvassers for, or agents of, the candidates, limiting the permissible expenditures of candidates, and requiring their sworn statements of the amounts actually disbursed. The result would be that the municipal elections, being entirely disassociated from all general issues, could take place in perfect freedom from such issues, and party Machines, which are generally built up around questions of national politics, and state or national issues, would as such count for little or nothing at the charter election. Thus, in charter elections at least, the vote could be had of men standing in perfect equality before the ballot-box as regards every detail of the machinery of election from beginning to end. All general issues being eliminated by the possibility of nominations independent of all partisan considerations, and it being possible to get the name of every candidate before every voter at the public expense, the army of paid workers would disappear as soon as their trade was made criminal, and they were deprived of their own votes. The Machines, and all that appertains to them, exist only because the law has not gone far enough. When it has gone further, and assumed the performance of all the essential functions of conducting an election, there will no longer be either reason, opportunity, or room for the Machine, and no occasion for assessing candidates or office-holders, for there will be no outlet for the money.

Where only two or three, and they partisan, candidates are in the field, it is only natural that the voter, since he has to determine the choice of evils, should vote for the candidate of the party with which he usually acts. Were the law first to provide the means for placing candidates in nomination, who shall occupy a position exactly as good as that occupied by the party candidates, and then separate the charter from the general election, the means will be found once and for all on the part of all public-spirited citizens for escaping the choice of evils, and for acting in municipal matters from a municipal point of view only, entirely independent of all state or national considerations. In order to make such a remedy as has been suggested of real service, it would, under present constitutional conditions, be well to apply it only to elections to city offices, and to make the elective officers as few as possible. Those officers now are the Mayor, the Comptroller, President of the Board of Aldermen, Recorder, Judges of the City Court, City Judges, the Aldermen, and the Civil Justices. The experience of such a law as reforming our municipal elections and our municipal government, might lead ultimately to its adoption for all state and county officers whatever, and work the reform which is needed throughout the entire State, though not so urgently needed as in our great cities. It may be said that these reforms are impossible. If so, I would reply in the words of Mr. John Morley: "Nearly all lovers of improvement are apt, in the heat of a generous enthusiasm, to forget that if all the world were ready to embrace their cause, their improvement could hardly be needed. It is one of the hardest conditions of things that the more numerous and resolute the enemies of reform, then the more unmistakably urgent the necessity for it."

APPENDIX I.

TABLE OF LICENSED SALOONS IN ASSEMBLY DISTRICTS.

ASSEMBLY DISTRICTS.	Class 1.	Class 2.	Class 3.	Class 4.	Class 5.	TOTALS.
First Assembly District........	4	10	923	88	47	1072
Second Assembly District.......	..	5	467	12	27	511
Third Assembly District........	3	8	309	20	28	368
Fourth Assembly District.......	..	..	174	2	27	203
Fifth Assembly District........	..	1	289	7	18	315
Sixth Assembly District........	..	1	232	2	53	288
Seventh Assembly District......	3	6	331	32	16	388
Eighth Assembly District.......	..	3	374	7	98	482
Ninth Assembly District	..	1	259	10	11	281
Tenth Assembly District........	1	1	315	3	48	368
Eleventh Assembly District.....	9	17	239	38	14	317
Twelfth Assembly District......	..	..	318	9	63	390
Thirteenth Assembly District...	..	1	200	19	15	235
Fourteenth Assembly District...	..	1	164	13	36	214
Fifteenth Assembly District....	..	..	439	5	23	467
Sixteenth Assembly District....	..	6	302	15	24	347
Seventeenth Assembly District..	..	4	196	34	14	248
Eighteenth Assembly District...	..	1	277	24	25	327
Nineteenth Assembly District...	..	7	381	64	28	480
Twentieth Assembly District....	..	2	252	15	18	287
Twenty-first Assembly District..	1	6	101	29	8	145
Twenty-second Assembly District	..	1	414	28	20	463
Twenty-third Assembly District.	..	..	516	26	44	586
Twenty-fourth Assembly District	..	1	301	9	106	417
Total........	21	83	7773	511	811	9199

```
Total number of licenses issued............... 9574
   "      "       "       "     existing............   9199
   "      "       "       "     closed..............    406
                                                       ─────
                                                       9605
                                                       9574
                                                       ─────
              Discrepancy...............          31
```

APPENDIX II.

The following tables show—

A. The elective offices in New York City.
B. The number of election officers for every state or municipal election in New York City.
C. The number of Assembly Districts and election districts, and the total of registered voters in each Assembly District, and the average of registered voters in each election district in New York City, for the year 1886.

A.

ELECTIVE OFFICERS.

Mayor.
Comptroller.
President of the Board of Aldermen.
Twenty-four Aldermen.
Sheriff.
County Clerk.
Register.
Four Coroners.
District Attorney.
Twenty-four Members of Assembly.
Seven Senators

Seven Justices of the Supreme Court.
Six Justices of the Superior Court.
Six Justices of the Court of Common Pleas.
Six Justices of the City Court.
Eleven District Court Civil Justices.
Recorder.
Judge of General Sessions.
City Judge.
Surrogate.

B.

ELECTION OFFICERS.

Year.	Number Election Districts.	Poll-clerks in each Dist.	Total Poll-clerks.	Inspectors of Election each Dist.	Total Inspectors Election.	Total Inspectors and Poll-clerks.
1884	712	2	1424	4	2848	4272
1885	712	2	1424	4	2848	4272
1886	812	2	1624	4	3248	4872

Duties of Inspectors of Elections.

There are four Inspectors of Election in each election district. They must meet and be in constant attendance at the designated place of registration and polling on the four appointed days of registration and on election-day. One of the four must be designated as chairman. Their duties are clearly set forth in a "Manual" issued by the Bureau of Elections, and are briefly as follows: They must register the names, etc., of all duly qualified voters who may apply for registration. The chairman must, at the close of each day's registration, deliver to the police-captain of the precinct in which the election district is located a list of the names, etc., of every person who registered on that day. 2d. They must keep six books, exact copies, of the names, etc., of the persons who register. 3d. They must receive and deposit the ballots of such registered voters on election-day, and allow no person to vote whose name is not on their registers. 4th. They must count and declare the vote in their election district, and return duly attested statements of the vote cast to the Clerk of the Board of Aldermen, the County Clerk, and the Chief of the Bureau of Elections.

Duties of Poll-clerks.

There are two poll-clerks in each election district. Their duties are also set forth in the "Manual" referred to, but are chiefly as follows: 1st. They must attend at the polling-place at the opening of the polls on election-day, and remain in constant attendance. 2d. They must each keep a poll list, and record therein the name of every person who votes. They must also keep two tally lists of the officers for which each person votes. 3d. They must sign both poll lists and tallies, after comparison, and return, within twenty-four hours after the close of the polls, one poll list and one tally to the Chief of the Bureau of Elections, one poll list to the County Clerk, and one tally to the Mayor.

APPENDIX II.

C.

1886.

Assembly Districts.	No. Election Districts.	Total registered voters.	Av. No. reg. voters each Election Dis.
First............	25	6,283	$251\frac{8}{25}$
Second.........	28	7,368	$263\frac{4}{28}$
Third...........	28	7,500	$267\frac{24}{28}$
Fourth..........	29	9,157	$315\frac{22}{29}$
Fifth............	29	7,058	$243\frac{11}{29}$
Sixth...........	29	8,671	299
Seventh........	35	8,838	$252\frac{18}{35}$
Eighth..........	31	8,961	$289\frac{2}{31}$
Ninth...........	32	9,863	$308\frac{7}{32}$
Tenth...........	31	9,816	$316\frac{20}{31}$
Eleventh........	25	6,342	$253\frac{17}{25}$
Twelfth.........	27	8,201	$303\frac{20}{27}$
Thirteenth......	34	9,281	$272\frac{33}{34}$
Fourteenth......	22	6,825	$310\frac{5}{22}$
Fifteenth.......	36	11,261	$312\frac{29}{36}$
Sixteenth.......	28	8,355	$298\frac{11}{28}$
Seventeenth....	42	12,821	$305\frac{11}{42}$
Eighteenth......	32	9,254	$289\frac{6}{32}$
Nineteenth......	43	13,842	$321\frac{39}{43}$
Twentieth.......	34	9,714	$285\frac{24}{34}$
Twenty-first.....	29	8,849	$305\frac{4}{29}$
Twenty-second..	58	17,359	$299\frac{17}{58}$
Twenty-third....	66	19,556	$296\frac{20}{66}$
Twenty-fourth...	39	10,586	$271\frac{17}{39}$
	812	23,5761	$290\frac{281}{812}$

Average registered per Assembly District........... $9823\frac{9}{24}$
Average No. Election Districts per Assembly District. $33\frac{20}{24}$

APPENDIX III.

I believe the general statement which I have made in the text to be entirely correct as to the decade immediately preceding the fall of the Tweed Ring, notwithstanding the fact that I find the following editorial article in the *New York Herald* for November 1, 1858, which will be found very interesting in this connection:

"The outlay which these candidates for public office have to make in the course of a campaign would form a very curious study, and its results would be quite suggestive. First, the nomination has to be paid for, and paid for liberally. The price, of course, depends upon the salary of the office, or the estimate of what it may be made to yield. It is known that $10,000 has been paid for a nomination to the Mayoralty, and a like sum for that to the Street Commissionership. Some people might possibly fail to see the great advantage to be derived from paying $10,000 for an office the salary of which for the whole term did not exceed $9000; but office-holders and office-seekers have a knack of reconciling this little anomaly in a mode profitable to themselves, but not so profitable to the community.

APPENDIX III.

The nomination being secured, it then becomes necessary to pay for the banners, for the music, for the torch-light processions, for the speakers, and the platforms on which they stand — for the artillery discharges, for the sky-rockets and Roman candles, for the notices in the Sunday newspapers, and for the enthusiasm generally. It costs about $2000 to be elected to the office of Coroner, a like sum to be a member of the Common Council, $5000 to get to Congress, $15,000 to be elected Street Commissioner or Sheriff, $20,000 to be elected Mayor, and so on in proportion to the estimated value of the post, or of what may be made out of it. Independently of the candidates for State offices and for Congress, we have in New York sixty-four candidates for county offices, whose aggregate outlay in the effort to get elected cannot fall far short of a quarter million of dollars. With the expenditure for the State and Congressional tickets, including the prices paid for nomination, the whole sum spent in this city on the election may be fairly set down at half a million of dollars. How public-spirited, generous, and munificent must be our politicians, or else how corrupt must be the conduct of our office-holders! The records of the Grand Jury room and of the criminal courts indicate pretty conclusively how the matter stands."

APPENDIX IV.

HOW THE ENGLISH LAW HAS WORKED.

For many years the English law, like our own, has been such that a fraud in polling or canvassing the vote was a practicable impossibility. Nevertheless, the elections continually miscarried because of the prevalence of corrupt practices and the enormous expenditure of money at the elections. It was to cure these evils that the Prevention of Corrupt Practices Act of 1883 and 1884 was passed. Now the value of legislation, like the value of a business project, can only be measured by actual results, and the best way to foretell what the result of the application to this country of the general principles of the English system will be, is to study what the effects of that system have been in England itself. The history of the elections of 1880 and 1886 shows a most marked contrast between the elections of the two years, and amounts to a demonstration of the efficiency of the law.

In 1880 an unusually large number of members of Parliament were unseated for corrupt practices at the elections. An investigation was made by a Royal Commission of twenty-four members. Among the seats contested was that of Alex. W. Hall, Conservative for Oxford. The Mayor of Oxford testified before the Commission that the majority of the electors always expected to be employed on election-day as clerks and messengers; and Mr. Hall's election agent swore that almost all of his papers were destroyed "because they would have disclosed quasi-corrupt transactions." At Canterbury the agent of the Liberal candidate who was defeated swore that his principal had deliberately given him money for the express purpose of buying up poor voters. Mr. Butler-Johnstone, the former Liberal member, swore that he was once elected by corrupt practices, and that at least 400 out of the 2700 voters in the constituency were corrupt.

At Macclesfield the agent of the Conservative candidate testified that he had bought up sixty Liberals at £5 per head and their beer; that to try to conduct an election without money was a farce; and that although he had only returned his expenses at £610, they had actually been £2590. There were 5700 votes polled, and this same witness swore that on one side or the other at least 4000 had been bribed. His candidate polled 2678, of which he, the agent, had bought and paid for 1863, at an average of six shillings and eightpence each, and had paid 550 others as clerks, messengers, and committeemen.

At Boston it appeared that twenty per cent. of the voters were employed as clerks, messengers, canvassers, committeemen, or what not. But it was at Sandwich that the most interesting showing was made. The special correspondent of the *New York World* summarized the evidence at the time, and I cannot do better than quote his carefully prepared article from the issue of November 28, 1880 :

"Sandwich, in the fair county of Kent, consists of the parishes of Deal, Walmer, St. Mary, St. Peter, St. Clement, and St. Bartholomew. Sandwich, with a population of 14,916 and a registration of 2115 electors, freemen, inhabitants rated for the relief of the poor and lodgers to the value of £10. It returns two members to Parliament. In 1832 both were Liberals; in 1835 the delegation was divided; in 1837 the Liberals regained the second seat, which they lost at a by-election in 1841; in 1847 two Liberals were elected; in 1852 the delegation was amicably divided; in 1857, in 1859, and in 1865 the Liberals elected both members; and though in 1866, at a by-election, the Conservative candidate just secured the vacant seat, at the general elections of 1868, 1874, and 1880 the Liberal members, Messrs. E. H. Knatchbull-Hugessen and H. A. Brassey, were returned. In 1874 the Liberals polled 1035 votes, and the Conservatives 764 ; and the Liberal majority was so large that in April last the Conservatives ran no candidates. In May, however, Mr. Knatchbull-Hugessen was elevated to

APPENDIX IV.

the peerage as Lord Brabourne, and for the vacant seat against Sir Julian Goldsmid, Liberal, the Conservatives put up Mr. C. H. Crompton-Roberts, a wealthy contractor, who carried the borough by 1145 to 705. The result was so manifestly obtained by irregular means that a petition was made, on which the Conservative member was unseated on the ground of bribery by his 'agents; Sir Julian's agents being similarly to blame, each side was ordered to pay its own costs, and the House was recommended to suspend the issue of a new writ until the extraordinary prevalence of corruption had been investigated.

"A Royal commission, composed of Mr. William Hayworth Holl, Q. C., and Messrs. Richard Edward Turner and Francis Henry Jeune, barristers, has been taking evidence in the doomed borough for several weeks past. Both candidates, their agents, and several hundred voters have been examined, and the story of an English Eatanswill is worth giving. I may prelude it by stating that the expenses at the uncontested election in April were £583, while in May those incurred by Mr. Crompton-Roberts were returned at £3153 5s. 3d., and those of Sir Julian Goldsmid at £888 13s. 1d., or something over $11 of your currency for each vote polled. But these figures, circumstantial as they are, do not represent the total expenditure; the third witness, Sir Julian's agent,

APPENDIX IV.

told how a single sum of £1500 had been brought down by the Liberals, gave it as his candid opinion that unless a man were prepared to spend £2000 it was idle for him to contest the borough, and declared that he had told Sir Julian at their first interview that £3000 would be needed to secure his election. Before the ballot all freemen used to receive £1 each when they went to the poll. Mr. Crompton-Roberts's solicitor admitted that corrupt practices prevailed extensively at the election. Then the Commissioners began to unearth these corrupt practices in detail. One Liberal agent spent £40 in treating and £51 in buying voters at from 15 shillings to £4 a head. A Conservative agent spent £390 in hiring public-houses as committee-rooms at £5 each; in all, the Conservatives had ninety-one 'headquarters'—one for every 12 voters. One spent £96 in bribery; another, £48; a third, £80; a fourth, £52, and so on down a long list. One enterprising publican let his house to the Conservatives and bribed for the Liberals. Another, who had been given £30, kept £22 19s. for himself, securing one other vote besides his own: he charged £10 for canvassing that voter. The members of the 'Bold Forty-two' got £3 13s. each from the Liberals and £3 each from the Conservatives, and one particularly bold Forty-twoer got £35 13s. in all by selling himself impartially to all canvassers. This, indeed, was the common practice; over fifty voters

APPENDIX IV.

came up in succession to swear that they had been bribed on both sides; one had been bought thrice. Several said regretfully that they should like to have another such job. The lowest price paid for voters was £3, with a further sum of £2 promised after the election; not a few witnesses said they hadn't yet received the £2, but still hoped to get it. One, a builder, declared that he had bribed at that election, and at every previous election, and 'would spend money again if he had a chance.' Refreshments were profusely distributed to the free and independent. One man spent £20, and 'treated every one he saw;' another spent £11, and so on. One landlord brought in a bill for ' 3 cwt. of rope and refreshments.' Altogether, the Conservatives spent between £2000 and £3000 on public-houses, and the Liberals £750—so small a sum, indeed, that the free and independent voters went to Sir Julian Goldsmid in person to ask where any of his beer was to be had. But the great device of this memorable election was—flags! The town was described by one witness as 'a forest of poles;' another said that people came many miles to see the display of bunting. There was one glorious pole from which twenty flags floated, with, at the mast-head, a huge pennant inscribed 'Our Illustrious Leaders,' and bearing the names of the members of the Cabinet. First, the flag and the pole are bought of voters at fancy prices; then a site on which to erect the pole is rented from a voter; then any number of voters are hired to put it up; and finally a number of watchers are engaged to protect it. One pole cost £25; it took thirty men three days to erect it, and two reliefs of watchers, each of six men, stood sentry over it at £2 apiece. One voter asked £30 for a site on which to plant a flag-staff, but came down to £2; another got £3 for 'watching' a flag—the 'watching' consisting in 'looking at it' when he went to bed and when he got up. One influential voter, whose annual rent is £46, got £84 for the use of five rooms of his house during two weeks. One man sold his vote twice, had his two children retained as messengers at £1 each, and received £1 for his services in 'walking up and down the street.' There were some 230 messengers employed; among them were boys of nine, who were paid 4s. 6d. a day. One snug British tradesman appeared who 'never altered his opinions—when there was an election he gave one vote to one side and one to the other; all he wanted was to speak the truth—he did not come there with a false tongue.' Another impartially dressed his shop in blue, distributed Liberal bills, and put blue bows on his children for one week, and the next hung out red banners on his outward walls, distributed Conservative documents, and put red neckties on his children. One voter grumbled because the Commissioners refused to allow him his expenses when subpœnaed a

APPENDIX IV.

second time after the discovery that he had been bribed twice, but had said nothing about the second bribery in his first examination. Another, who had sold himself for £6, clamored for 5s. for loss of time in testifying to his shame. Another, a journeyman boat-builder, demanded first-class travelling expenses. One agent swore to having received—from 'a short, dark man' whom he did not know—a sum of £1000 or £1300; when recalled upon the discovery that the amount was £1700 it came out that there had been 'such a rush to get it' that he had not been able to count it before it was divided up. In all about 900 of the 1850 voters swore to having been bribed. One agent declared that there were not 300 persons in Deal who did not have money, that sixty per cent. of the electors were venal, and that things had changed since the old times, when from £20 to £30 was paid for a vote to a limited class of corrupt electors, since 'now it was a general thing, and he could hardly go into a house but the people asked what they were to have.' If money was one side, the candidate on the other would, he said, stand no chance; and besides having the money, the Conservatives announced that if they were defeated they would never contest the borough again, so that the residents, terrified at this prospect, elected Mr. Crompton-Roberts, so as to compel the Liberals to put him out at the next election.

APPENDIX IV.

"The evidence of the two candidates was deeply interesting. Sir Julian Goldsmid said that on going to Sandwich his first ominous experience was hearing the universal remark: 'We were afraid we were not going to have a contest.' The Liberal agent told him it would cost about £2500 to carry the borough, and that the custom of the locality was to pay cash. Sir Julian spent £2230, or nearly thrice the amount returned to Parliament—the bulk of it, £1500, being furnished by a contractor for public works at Rochester and Sheerness, who said that he had 'generally paid Sir Julian's registration expenses, his subscriptions and such like.' The money was sent in gold on a verbal message delivered by a second person, and was given to a third person with whom the contractor was not acquainted, and who merely signed his initials to an unstamped and undated receipt! Sir Julian found during his second day's canvassing that the Liberals were only running him to have a contest, and intended to defeat him; that the amount of fictitious employment was 'enormous;' that tradesmen were being bought on all sides with orders for goods; that strangers asked him in the streets for money—hence he began taking notes for a petition before the election had taken place, and the day after it was held consulted with his friends, who declared it his duty to the public to have the borough disfranchised. 'It was something dreadful,' said the baronet, 'to have to go througn what I went through, and my main reason for petitioning was that no other candidate should be placed in my position.' He was threatened with personal violence; one voter, a leading Liberal, declared on the stand before the Commission that after finding out how 'mean' his candidate was (in pressing the petition) he would gladly vote to have him drowned! It was offered by the Conservatives that if Sir Julian would withdraw the petition and save the place from risk of disfranchisement, Mr. Crompton-Roberts would resign and Sir Julian would be allowed to walk over for the vacancy, and be paid his expenses at both elections and on the petition. Mr. Foord, the contractor already alluded to, said it cost him about £560 a year for party expenses. The £1500 went to Sandwich in May; in July Sir Julian thanked him for sending the money; in September he said he would repay it shortly, when he had some money coming in, and Mr. Foord said, 'Pay when you like.' October 20th Sir Julian sent him a check, but the check had not yet been put through the bank.

"But, oh, what a delightful witness Mr. Crompton-Roberts was! He told his agent that it was hardly fair to Sir Julian to engage so many public-houses, but the agent assured him that there would be enough left for the Liberals. He told his agent that he was bothered by people catching hold of him in the street and asking if they might not have some flags, and the agent said, 'Flags are illegal, and I cannot authorize any until the other side start it.' Hearing that Sir Julian was to be made a Forester, Mr. Crompton-Roberts thought he 'had better become one likewise;' and 'having understood that it was usual for new members to stand glasses round, asked the President's permission to order them,' whereupon Right Worthy—or whatever it is—Brother Goldsmid remarked that that was 'sailing very near the wind,' the law about treating being very rigid. On the Bank Holiday Mr. Crompton-Roberts gave a regatta, at which every boat got a money prize, and the townsfolk were all admitted free to the pier to see it. When he heard that only £20 would be expended for the fireworks on this holiday, Mr. Crompton-Roberts told his butler that he had often spent more than that for fireworks on the birthday of one of his children, and if the butler feared the display was going to be shabby he was to add what money he thought necessary. During the whole time he was in the borough Mr. Crompton-Roberts only saw 'one man a little gone,' and he was 'astonished' when he received the petition with its allegations. He could not believe them, and was further 'astonished' when his solicitor informed him that there must be some fire where there was so much smoke. The Conservative candidate

APPENDIX IV.

asked piteously 'If the borough was to be won by illegal means, why was I made to work harder than I ever did in my life for a fortnight? My agent, gentlemen, had my complete confidence, and I was like a child in his hands.' Poor Mr. Crompton-Roberts had to go round making speeches with a bit off of the top of one of his teeth, which made it agony for him to speak, but his inexorable agent refused to let him stop, and declared he was going to carry the election if he killed the candidate. Mr. Crompton-Roberts spent £6500 on the election, this sum not including his personal expenses or his petition costs, and thought 'this had been done economically, as he had always thought an election cost something like £10,000.' It is but just to say that he scattered much money in a manner that was ludicrous rather than corrupt; he 'tipped' his sons lavishly; he gave money freely to personal friends in gratitude for their expressions of hopefulness and sympathy; and he forced a £20 note on his governess for showing an interest in his candidature. He gave £18 to one local charity and £5 to another—the Foresters' Widow and Orphan Fund; by-the-way, his 'glasses round' on his election to the fraternity cost him £12. His house-keeper was liberal in distributing sums of from 2s. to 10s. to poor people who passed his house; his chemist got one order of £8 for soda-water alone; it took four butchers and five poulterers to supply the family with meat and poultry. Here are some extracts from his canvassing-book:

"'1. W. H.—Paralyzed; wants help to get change of air and rides out.

"'2. G. M.—Wants better pension.

"'3. D. B.—Very favorable, but poor.

"'4. T. J.—Promised; wants a little drop.

"'5. J. T.—Wants liquoring.

"'6. W. R.—Wants cash.

"'7. G. C.—Wants much assistance; had much illness in the house; half a year's rent at $3s.=£3$ $18s.$

"'8. J. T.—Wife wants liquoring up.

"'9. T. H. S.—Mother wants a liquor up.

"'10. G. T.—Some Brahee sugar powder.

"'11. T. S.—Expenses to Ramsgate to be paid; can bring two others.'

"When examined as to these entertaining entries, Mr. Crompton-Roberts declared that No. 1 'made that statement, and seemed to think he had a claim;' that he told No. 2 he had no right to ask a candidate to get him an increased pension; that the note about No. 3 was 'a statement of his case,' and not a hint about corrupting him; that No. 4 was 'a liquory kind of fellow,' and so on."

All this was in 1880. Every one familiar with English history is more or less acquainted with the corruption which prevailed in the earlier days, when, in his will,

APPENDIX IV.

the Right Hon. George Venables made a bequest of five thousand pounds to his "dear son-in-law towards the purchase of a seat in Parliament;" when elections were openly bought and sold; and when, for instance, one thousand pounds were offered for a single vote, as was once done at Malmesbury. But in 1880 better things were to have been expected, and although very great improvements had been made on the election methods and morals of the early part of the century, corruption was still rife, because of the numberless ways of cloaking it which were offered on every hand. It was to cure this evil that Sir Henry James's Act was passed. *When it was under discussion it was freely predicted that it must fail of its purpose because the evils complained of were not such as could be reached by legislation.* How admirably the law has succeeded, however, may be seen from the following summary of the official returns of election expenses for 1886, published in the *Pall Mall Gazette*, under the title "The Cheapest Election on Record:"

"The official return showing the cost of the election of 1886 which has just been published is drawn up in the same way, and shows the same general features as the similar return for the election of 1885. This earlier return was analyzed so fully in our columns (September

6, 1886) from the point of view of the Corrupt Practices Act that we need not dwell on this matter again. It will suffice to state generally that every conclusion we then drew is confirmed by the experience of a second election under the Act. The expenses have been reduced all round by at least one-half; and not only so, but as a rule those who pay highest no longer poll heaviest. On the contrary, it would probably be found that the unsuccessful candidates throughout the kingdom spent considerably more than the elected members. This is notably the case in Ireland, where Parnellites generally beat their opponents by double the number of votes and at half the cost. As another point of resemblance between this election and the last, we may notice that Northampton still retains its honorable position of being the cheapest seat going; Mr. Labouchere and Mr. Bradlaugh paid only 6$d.$ a vote—a reduction of 2$d.$ on last time.

"But indeed the salient feature of this election throughout on the financial side is its cheapness. Before illustrating this point, however, in detail, we may give, in the same form as on the last occasion, the actual figures. The following table is compiled from the Bluebook; in the 'total expenses' column shillings and pence are omitted throughout—this explains the apparent inaccuracy in the totals:

APPENDIX IV.

	Total Expenses.	Cost per Vote.	Total Expenses.	Cost per Vote.
	£	s. d.	£	s. d.
England:				
Counties	284,989	5 2		
Boroughs	203,331	3 1		
Universities	305	2 8		
Total England			488,626	4 0
Wales:				
Counties	18,801	4 11		
Boroughs	8,255	4 6		
Total Wales			27,056	4 10
Scotland:				
Counties	55,629	5 8		
Burghs	26,983	3 3		
Universities	245	— —		
Total Scotland			82,858	4 7
Ireland:				
Counties	20,852	2 5		
Boroughs	4,142	2 2		
Universities	549	2 10		
Total Ireland			25,544	2 5
Total United Kingdom	....	....	624,086	4 0

" The total cost of electing the present Parliament was, it will thus be seen, £624,086, that of electing the last £1,026,645, showing a decrease of over £400,000. This enormous reduction was, however, partly due, of course, to the simple fact that there were many more uncontested elections in 1886 than in 1885. In 1885 there were 641 contests, in 1886 only 442. Now, uncontested elections do not cost nothing, but they cost very little. We shall not be far wrong, therefore, if, for the purpose of comparison, we ignore the cost in these cases, and

APPENDIX IV.

bring the figures of the two elections to a common measure on the basis of the number of contests. On this showing the cost of the 1886 election would—at the rate of the 1885 one—have been £707,920; it was £624,086 —leaving even so a reduction of over £80,000. The reduction will perhaps be brought out more clearly by the following comparative table:

	Total Cost.	Average cost per contest.	Cost per vote.				
			England.	Wales.	Scotland.	Ireland.	United Kingdom.
	£	£	s. d.	s. d.	s. d.	s. d.	s. d.
1885..	1,026,645	1,601	4 4	5 7	5 8	2 9	4 5
1886..	624,086	1,411	4 0	4 10	4 7	2 5	4 0

" It is a reduction, it will be seen, of about 10 per cent. all along the line. Absolutely and relatively to the number of contests alike the election of 1886 is the cheapest on record. 'Unionists' may fairly boast that although they carried the Union in 1800 by bribery and corruption, they 'maintained' it in 1886 on the cheap."

As was pointed out by the *New York Evening Post*, the most significant fact disclosed by the English elections of 1886 is "*that the grand total of expenditure by candidates is only a little more than one-half of the grand total allowed by the law.*" The fact is, that competitive expenditure, as it exists in this country to-day, must continue because of the essential nature of all competi-

APPENDIX IV. 149

tion of this kind to increase the outlay of all candidates whatever in a steady progression. Expenditure begets expenditure; and assuming that a candidate is permitted to spend as much as he pleases, his competitors will always be impelled to spend as much as he or suffer the consequences. It is in this way that certain districts get hopelessly debauched. Thus, when Mr. L. P. Morton first ran for Congress in New York City, his district was flooded with money; and when, subsequently, Mr. Roswell P. Flower and Mr. W. W. Astor, both millionaires, ran in the same district, the competitive expenditure was such as to produce almost complete demoralization. The history of the English law shows that where the permissible expenditure is limited the opposite effect is produced, and that candidates no longer being allowed to test their popularity by the length of their purses, find no motive or incentive to spend even the moderate sums allowed by law. In 1880, with about 3,000,000 voters in 419 constituencies, there was spent over £3,000,000 or $15,-000,000; while in 1886, with an increased number of voters, there was expended but £624,086, or about $3,000,-000. In 1880 ninety-five petitions alleging corrupt practices were presented, while only two were presented in 1885 and only one in 1886. To quote the *New York Nation*, referring to these facts, " Corruption in politics has been practically abolished." The most interesting fact of all, however, is that already referred to, that the expenditure did not reach the permitted limit; commenting on which fact the *London Daily News* says, "The first thing which they (the figures) prove is the complete success of Sir Henry James's Act. The chief feature of that Act was that it laid down a maximum expenditure, to exceed which would be a corrupt practice voiding the seat. The experts said that the maximum was placed too low—the experience of the last election demonstrates that, as usual, the experts were wrong, and that on the contrary the maximum is too high. It would be possible to reduce by at least one-fourth the sums allowed by law without in any way starving the elections. There are very few cases in which the maximum was reached."

THE END.

Augsburg College
George Sverdrup Library
Minneapolis, Minnesota 55404